CONFRONTATION

The Existential Thought
of Rabbi J. B. Soloveitchik

CONFRONTATION

The Existential Thought of Rabbi J. B. Soloveitchik

by

ZVI KOLITZ

KTAV PUBLISHING HOUSE, INC.
HOBOKEN, NEW JERSEY 07030

Library of Congress Cataloging-in-Publication Data

Kolitz, Zvi, 1913-
 Confrontation : the existential thought of Rabbi J.B. Soloveitchik
/ by Zvi Kolitz.
  p.   cm.
 ISBN 0-88125-431-2
 1. Soloveitchik, Joseph Dov--Views on man. 2. Man (Jewish
theology) 3. Judaism and philosophy. 4. Spiritual life--Judaism.
5. Sin (Judaism) I. Title.
BM755.S6144K65 1992
296.3'2'092--dc20   92-32034
                                                           CIP

Manufactured in the United States of America

To my wife Mathilde
and my children
Dalia
Elinoar
Jonathan
with Love

Contents

5. **Sin-Sickness and** *Teshuvah*

6. **Sin as Spiritual Pathology**

7. **Kant Would Not Have Understood My Grandfather**

Acknowledgment

The author wishes to express his thanks to the "Jewish Publication Society" of Philadelphia for help rendered in securing the rights to extensively quote from "The Halakhic Man."

To me, there is no division between "rigid halakah" and "flowing prophetism;" between the sobriety of the Law and the intoxication of poesy.

Rabbi Nehemiah Nobel

Preface

On various occasions, listening to lectures or sermons by modern young Orthodox rabbis who mention with justified pride their having studied under Rav Soloveitchik at Yeshiva University, I have been struck by the almost total lack of reference to the Rav's philosophy of existence. The opinions of the Rav cited by the speakers are almost invariably on halakhic matters or, more rarely, on his homiletical interpretations, and hardly ever touch on problems relating to his philosophy of life, to which his halakhic philosophy has added such an unmistakably existential dimension.

Since Rav Soloveitchik is undoubtedly the preeminent contemporary Jewish thinker and the single most influential interpreter of the spirit of Judaism in the last half century, why is there such apparent reluctance on the part of his most ardent disciples to discuss the ontological implications of his thought?

The explanation, it seems to this author, must lie in the understandable, though much less justifiable, reluctance of young spiritual leaders to expound an idea which is, at bottom, on a collision course with the general trend that for two centuries or so has seen the ubiquitous "pursuit of happiness" as an almost constitutionally guaranteed right. The notion that one is supposed to be happy just as one is supposed to be free is regarded by the Rav as simply unfair to man, who was created "to create himself" through a constant pursuit of *meaning* even at the price of happiness. Man, as seen by the Rav, justifies his existence by creating himself throughout his lifetime from an inner *tohu vavohu*. This, however, has a beneficial side, for it is "torn man who is the creator." Yet man's tornness, though beneficial, can be a terrifying experience. Even those who experience it find it difficult to expound, let alone

xiii

admit. The Rav, however, does both—expound and admit—a rare occurrence in the spiritual confessionals of great-souled men.

To those who prefer cheerfulness to meaningfulness—a cheerfulness which is ultimately conducive to vacuity—the Rav's thought is, of course, a rude awakener. But even those who regard it as a reliable pointer of the way would hesitate to admit that the way pointed out by the Rav must often be trodden with bleeding feet, with an aching heart, and in howling storms. It is, after all, a way which runs in the opposite direction from the well-trodden paths preachified by the pietistic distributors of grace, the religious pacifiers and dispensers of quick soul-saving formulas. Only now, with the collapse of all those happiness-promising social systems throughout the world, on the one hand, and with a helpless psychiatry on the wane, on the other, do we realize, with Soren Kierkegaard, that "systems are only for God." The Torah, a system which attests to its Divine origin ("halakhic man doesn't need any proof that God exists; the Torah proves it"), cannot but abhor vacuums—the diagnosed malaise of all man-made systems. The Torah, in contradistinction, covers not just the whole man, but the idea of man's wholeness even in his creative tornness. Thus, it is precisely the quality which its detractors refer to as narrowness that is, in actuality, the dialectical stepping stone to the *merhav-yah*, the grandiose vistas of wholeness of which the psalmist speaks so passionately, and which are almost invariably preceeded by the *min hametzar*, "out of the narrow straits."

Antithesis? Of course! Immense creative powers, the Rav argues, are vested in the antithesis. Religion itself does not offer a synthesis. The friction caused by the clash between the thesis and the antithesis is a source of life-giving and soul-restoring energy. Why, even "the energy of sin points upward!" No other Jewish thinker has dared to spell this out, and it is certainly too bold—as bold as it is profound—to be explained in a sermon. It would be equally difficult to explain the Rav's contention that religion doesn't necessarily answer mans questions; that, if anything, "it deepens the problems, but never intends to solve them." To say, as the Rav does, that "the beauty of religion reveals itself to man not in solutions, but in problems, not in harmony, but in the constant conflicts of diversified forces and trends," is not a promise of easy salvation, but a call for transformation, which, in turn, is impossible without self-confrontation.

Transformation, as the Rav sees it, is first and foremost an invitation to a knowledge, an understanding, which one does not acquire in a synagogue, but in a *bet medrash* (house of study), for it is the *bet medrash*, he maintains, not the synagogue, which has molded the spirit of Jewry down the ages. To convey this message to predominantly synagogue Jews, however sincerely religious they may be, is as difficult as explaining to them the awesome dialectical gap between existential loneliness, to which the Rav does not hesitate to admit, and "the touch of His hand"—God's hand—on his shoulders, of which the Rav speaks with equal certainty. But it is precisely this dichotomy which renders the Rav's thought, today more than ever before, so intensely reflective of life's endlessly perplexing antinomies.

Many people today, young people in particular, tired as they are of the seductions of vulgar materiality and of the reductionist confusing of security with happiness, would rather be caught up in the wider world of confrontational thought than in the thoughtless world of a painless nonconfrontation. No, it is not a "happier" self—"happy" as commonly understood—which one is called upon to be transformed into, but a *wider* self—"a wider self," to quote William James, "through whom comes a saving experience." Even painful growth, as long as it is growth, is a saving experience. If people were hesitant to draw too close to the Rav's thought, it was not because they felt—and rightly so—that they were dealing with an oceanic soul, as stormy and serene as an ocean, but because they did not trust their ability to brave it. Little did they realize that the Rav never dared them to brave it, but to swim it—nay, to *learn* to swim.

The following presentation is an invitation to swim.

Rabbi Norman (Nahum) Lamm, the president of Yeshiva University and one of Rav Soloveitchik's most outstanding disciples, was kind enough to read the manuscript of this book and make some pertinent observations and suggestions for which I am profoundly grateful.

There is, however, one point on which the author begs to differ with his master. Rabbi Lamm avers that to portray the Rav as an opponent of Hasidism is, in his words, "an oversimplification." That may very well be so, for oversimplification is sometimes a pedagogical tool used by an author, fully aware of the sensitive nature of the subject at hand, who is seeking to summarize what is most complex in the thought of a Gaon he is trying to explore.

The Rav's thought in such matters is the result of his keen observations of great spiritual currents in Judaism, not only of the original intentions which underlie them. In this sense, one might say that the Rav is, so to speak, a pragmatist. It is this pragmatism, however, which may redeem my "oversimplification" from the pitfalls of inaccuracy. It would not be inaccurate to say, for example, that while there can be little doubt that some Hasidic masters fit perfectly into the Rav's grand vision of the Halakhic Man and Halakhic mind, the majority of the Hasidim—the learned minority notwithstanding—do not exactly regard these attributes as a Rebbe's "claim to fame." While seeking a religion of ecstasy, they often overlook the theonomy of pathos, which the Halakhic dimension of depth is all about.

Dr. Lamm mentioned to me that many years ago he saw and transcribed a manuscript in Hebrew by the Rav. The manuscript was entitled "Ish ha-Elohim." It was never published as such (but may have subsequently found its way into other of his works). In other words, the *homo religiosus* and the Halakhic Man are superseded by the Man of God. If the Rav has indeed written about this—and this author has tried in vain to locate the original manuscript—there can be little doubt that on that exalted level the Gaon of Vilna and Rabbi Shneur Zalman of Liadi are no longer opponents.

August 10, 1992

1

Existential Judaism

THE HALAKHIC MAN OF TOTAL INVOLVEMENT

Matthew Arnold, the inspired nineteenth-century English writer and thinker, quotes a felicitous remark by Thomas Carlyle, another great Englishman, which in a few words defines the distinction between Hebraism and Hellenism. "Socrates," Carlyle said, "is terribly at ease in Zion." To this Arnold comments: "Hebraism—and here is the source of its wonderful strength—has always been severely preoccupied with an awful sense of the impossibility of being at ease in Zion" (read: the world); of the difficulties which oppose themselves to man's pursuit or attainment of that perfection of which Socrates talks so hopefully and, from this point of view, so glibly. It is all very well to talk of getting rid of one's ignorance, of seeing things in their reality, of seeing them in their beauty; "but how is this to be achieved when there is something which thwarts and spoils all our efforts?"

"This something," Arnold replies, "is sin."

We shall return to the question of sin, as viewed by Reb Yosef Ber Soloveitchik (to whom we shall henceforth refer, for the sake of brevity, as the Rav) as we proceed. The question of sin, as seen by the Halakhah and classified by the Rav, will be better understood if we concentrate at this early stage of our inquiry, on *existential uneasiness* as the characteristic that differentiates Hebraism from Hellenism and, for that matter, the Rav from some existentialist thinkers who treat religion as a tranquilizer.

It is obvious that what Matthew Arnold perceives in this definition of Hebraism is the thought, shared by William Barrett and other philosophers, that deep within biblical man lurks a certain

1

uneasiness which is not to be found in the conceptions of man given us by the great Greek philosophers. This uneasiness, according to Arnold, arises from the Hebrew preoccupation with *doing*, as opposed to the Greek concern with *knowing*. Right conduct, Arnold writes, is the prime concern of the Hebrew; right knowing, of the Greek. Duty and strictness of conscience are paramount things in the life of the Hebrew; for the Greek it was the spontaneous and luminous play of the intellect.

William Barrett, the American philosopher, rightly remarks (in *Irrational Man*) that Arnold seeks to tie in the uneasiness of biblical man—the prophets were, after all, the first to warn against being at ease in Zion—with his main thesis, which is the distinction between moral practice and intellectual culture, by introducing the idea of sin. But the sinfulness that man experiences in the Bible, as expressed in the Psalms or in the Book of Job, cannot be confined to a supposed compartment of the individual's being that has to do with his moral acts. "This sinfulness, as perceived by Biblical man, pervades his whole being. It is indeed man's being, insofar as his feebleness and finiteness as a creature, that stands, so to speak, naked in the presence of God. This idea of man's finiteness takes us beyond the distinctions of practice and theory, morality and knowledge, toward the center from which all such distinctions stem."

For Hellenism that center was reason. For Hebraism it was the law. The Greeks gave us science and technology; the Hebrews gave us the law. "No other people," in Barrett's words, "not the Chinese, not the Indians, nor the Hindus produced theoretical science, and its discovery and invention by the Greeks has been what has distinguished Western civilization from other civilizations of the globe. In the same way, the uniqueness of Western religion is due to its Hebrew source, and the religious history of the West is the long story of the varying fortunes and mutations of the spirit of Hebraism."[1]

Barrett mentions other vital distinctions between Hebraism and Hellenism, distinctions which, in our view, would make it obvious

---

1. The first biblical prophecy, that of Noah, addresses itself, with amazing precision, to this future development: "May God enlarge—or beautify—Yaphet," whose son, we are told right there, is Yavan (Greece), "but He will dwell in the tents of Shem," whose son, we are told right there, is Eber (Hebrew).

that contrary to Hellenism, Judaism indeed represents—concerned as it is with the whole man and his destined "uneasiness in Zion"—an existentialist world-view. Take *detachment*, for example. To the Hebrews it was an impermissible state of mind, while the realm of eternal essences—not the essence of existence but the existence of essences—was not only typical of Greek thought, but was well-nigh impossible to get involved with without a detached intellect. Plato had words of praise for such an intellect, which becomes "a spectator of all time and all existence." The Greek ideal of the theoretical intellect as the highest human type, who from the vantage point of eternity can survey, like a spectator, all time and existence, is altogether foreign to the Hebrew spirit—a spirit which is passionately committed to its own moral stature in its confrontation with God. It is not in vain that the Greeks invented the theater. In the theater we are spectators of an action in which we ourselves are not involved. The Hebraic emphasis, by everlasting contrast, is on *commitment*—the passionate involvement of man, with his body and soul, flesh and spirit—with his offspring, family, tribe, and God. "A man abstracted from such involvements," Barrett writes in truth, "would be, to Hebrew thought, but a pale shade of the actual, existing human person."

There are, of course, other significant distinctions between the Hebrew and Greek world-views—views which, as both Heinrich Heine and Georg Brandes rightly observed, define the two major trends in world culture to this very day. The Greeks "invented" logic. To the Greeks man was "the animal of the connected logical discourse," i.e., a "logical animal." The Hebrews regarded common logic with suspicion, for it does not touch upon the ultimate issues of life. The treatment which Scripture accords to the "logical" friends of Job is typical: the Almighty does not concur with "logical" Amen-sayers. There are ultimate issues of life which transpire in a depth that language can never reach and logic never perceive.

Contrary to the Greek notion of beauty and goodness as things that are identical or at least coincidental, the Hebrew sense of sin is too much aware of the galling and refractory aspects of human existence to make this easy identification of the good and the beautiful. Biblical man was too aware of his imperfection to fall prey to the easy lure of the good as identical with the beautiful.

These two main differences are enough, in our view, to make clear the central issues that inform the Greek and Hebrew views of man. Barrett summarizes it very succinctly: "The features of Hebraic man are those which existential philosophy has attempted to exhume and bring to the reflective consciousness of our time, a time in which as a matter of historical happening, the Hebraic religion (which means Western religion) no longer retains its meaningful validity for the mass of mankind."

THE RIFT BETWEEN LIFE AND SPIRIT

The equation of Hebraism with existentialism may surprise many, particularly those who associate existentialism with a novel intellectual fashion which originated, as many believe, in post-World War II France and was associated with the name of Jean-Paul Sartre. Soren Kierkegaard, who tried almost a century-and-a-half ago to lay the foundations of religious existentialism, was hardly known to the followers of French intellectual fashions, and the fashion in question suddenly assumed in the minds of many people the hue of a bohemian ferment brewing on an alienated Left Bank. It was also associated, for some reason, with particular nightclub hangouts, special hairdos, and a style of dress bespeaking a pronounced "Je m'en fous." That was, anyway, what many regarded as the outward appearance of existentialism. It also had an inner core of depth and darkness which some used as a conviction and others as a contrivance. Sartre, Camus and Simone de Beauvoir were not only distinguished literary figures by any standard; they were also fashionable personages worthy of emulation. Some Americans were intrigued by the message of existentialism, particularly since it lent some kind of philosophical respectability to experiences like anxiety, despair and alienation to which Americans were as ashamed to admit as to a social disease. In addition, there was, in post-World War II America, a confrontation of sorts with the question of evil on a scale Americans had never known before. The USA which never knew the political power of evil as did the Europeans—Sartre was the first to point it out to American friends—was suddenly compelled, at least on the level of thought, to revise some of its notions on being "at ease in Zion." The accepted pietistic notion of evil as "nothing but the other side of good" no longer worked, sermon-mongers notwithstanding.

The rift between life and the spirit expressed itself not only in the growing number of people seeking psychiatric help, but in the equally growing number of people who could no longer accept the recipes of "easy grace" offered in particular by Christian theology. The question of the place of individual human creativity in a world in which the soul is supposed to be saved or damned by a deterministic baptismal act has bothered many thinking Christians, particularly in the post–World War II era, when it became known how many so-called "saved souls" had participated in the extermination of the Jews. This question had been bothering Christian thinkers for centuries. Thus Pascal, himself no friend of the Jews, was tormented all his life by the question of whether the individual human factor has any creative role in the Christian domain. Pascal's great problem was whether the initiation of the religious relationship is placed entirely in God or "whether man's creativity is called upon." Three hundred years later there arose another great Frenchman who dared spell out the question without fear or mercy. Albert Camus's antipathy for religion, i.e., Christianity, was based on a conviction that human helplessness in this world was a basic Christian notion. Christianity, Camus argued, lacks a social stance and preaches an accommodation of sorts with a world of injustice, for in the Christian view the world is, in any event, consigned to the Devil, since "my kingdom is not of this world." Christianity, Camus claimed, is indifferent to human suffering. It keeps man from total involvement in his time and from regarding the agony of the human experience as a call for action. Camus thus saw here an attempt to emasculate human creativity and to hamstring human responsibility by Divine sanction, as it were. "Such a God," Camus declared, "must be dethroned."

Both Pascal and Camus questioned the place of individual human creativity in Christianity. Judaism's answer to this question is unequivocal; it is also basic to the Rav's existential thought. As he writes (in part 2 of *The Halakhic Man*,) "The most fundamental principle of all is that man must create himself. It is this idea which Judaism introduced into the world."

THE IMAGE OF GOD AND THE IMAGE OF MAN

If man was created to create himself, He who created him for this purpose could not possibly have done it without providing man with a blueprint that would tell him how to go about creating himself. This blueprint is the Torah. The need which the Rav felt, toward the end of World War II, when the greatest outburst of unrestrained evil in history was barely over, to present the blueprint for human self-creation in existential terms was undoubtedly due to what he had seen in the unfolding Shoah, namely, the most terrifying manifestation of the animalization of the image of man. And, indeed, the Rav's motto, "It is either the Divine Image or a beast of prey," sounded toward the end of the war as a summary of the human condition.

Nicholas Berdyaev writes in *The Fate of Man*: "There may have been a time when the image of man, his truly human nature, was not yet revealed—man was in a sort of potential state. This was the case in the past. But now we face something quite different: The image of man has been shaken, and it has begun to disintegrate after it *was* revealed."

Many thoughtful people were and still are tormented by the question, Where was God when the image of man—man created in His image—was disintegrating? This question, however, is not as central to the Rav's inquiry as the other one the Shoah raises, Where was man?

Aware as he must have been that the image of man that was disintegrating was not only that of secular man, but also that of the so-called religious man, the Rav, going as he does in the footsteps of Maimonides, saw the need, as the war drew to a close, to draw a clear distinction between the homo religiosus and the halakhic man. Time and again does the Rav come back to this distinction in his seminal work *The Halakhic Man*, and there was a good reason for this. To halakhic man, the law was an existential experience, while to the homo religiosus, religion in general was mostly an afterthought or a practice by rote. It is not in vain that Maimonides, in his famous parable of the palace, dealing with the diverse ways of seeking and finding God, says that "those who desire to arrive at the palace, and enter it, but have never yet seen it, are the mass of religious people, the multitude that observe the Divine commandments but are ignorant'' (*Guide* 3:51). The Rav draws a distinction even between the *learned* mystic and the halakhic man. He could not, after all, have overlooked the fact that many "religious" people in Nazi-occupied Europe saw no contradiction between the church to which they belonged and the murderously idolatrous movement with which they collaborated. Pope Pius XII, whose Nazi sympathies were well known, was also known as a mystic, Alas!

The Rav thus defines a clear, revolutionary distinction, unique in religious literature, between the homo religiosus even as a "mystic" and the halakhic man. And the essence of what distinguishes the halakhist from the religionist is this: while the homo religiosus, as known to other religions too, craves to *rise up* from the vale of tears and the concrete, bitter reality; and aspires to extricate himself from the narrow straits of empirical existence and emerge into the wide spaces of a pristine, transcendental existence, halakhic man longs to bring *transcendence* into the valley of the shadow and transform it into a land of the living. "Halakhic man," the Rav writes, "wishes to purify this world, not to escape it. . . . His goal is not flight into another world which is wholly good, but rather bringing down that eternal world into the midst of our world." As the Rav elaborates on this crucial subject, he does not hesitate to equate facile mysticisms with escapism. "The homo religiosus," the Rav continues, clearly referring to some fashionable mysticisms, "his glance fixed upon the higher realms, forgets all too frequently the lower realms and becomes ensnared in the sins of ethical inconsistency and hypocrisy." "See" the Rav exclaims unhesitatingly, "what many religions have done to this world on account of their yearning to break through the bounds of concrete reality and escape into the sphere of eternity. They have been so intoxicated by their dreams of an exalted supernal existence that they have failed to hear the cries of 'them that dwell in houses of clay' (Job 4:19)—the sighs of orphans, the moans of the destitute. Had they not desired to unite with infinity and merge with transcendence, they might have been able to do something to aid the widow and the orphan, to save the oppressed from the hand of the oppressor. There is nothing so physically and spiritually destructive as diverting one's attention from this world. And, by contrast, how courageous is halakhic man, who does not flee from this world, who does not seek to escape to some pure, supernal realm; Halakhic man craves to bring down the Divine Presence and holiness into the midst of the finite, earthly existence.''

In other words, to use an expression of Abraham Joshua Heschel's, "Beware of those whose God is in heaven!" The Torah is here to bring Him, as it were, down to earth.

The task of bringing God down to earth encompasses and invigorates the whole man, not just part of him, and it does not promise any easy way to achieve it. There is no such thing as "easy grace," just as there is no such thing as "laid back" religion of cosy immanence. There is not even any such thing as a shortcut to God by means of easy repentance. The Rav speaks harshly not only of those who seek refuge from existential problems in easy religion, but of those who seek there an escape from cultural burdens and scientific "future shocks." I know of no other contemporary thinker who puts it quite so bluntly.

The advocates of easy religion, as the Rav says (in "The Halakhic Man"), wish to exploit the rebellious impulse against knowledge which surges from time to time in the soul of the man of culture; the frequent yearnings to be freed from the bonds of culture—that daughter of knowledge—which weighs heavily on man with its yoke of questions, doubts, and problems; the perplexity which creates in him the desire to escape from the turbulence of life to a quiet, still, magical island and there to devote himself to the ideals of beauty, naturalness, and vitality. This is the illusory island of facile religion which the Rav attacks without mercy. We are all too familiar with it in America. A glimpse into the appalling shallowness of the Sunday morning religious-comedy hours featuring some TV evangelist is enough to make one shudder at the terrible simplifiers of a dimension which was once regarded as *the* dimension of depth. Those so-called spiritual leaders of all denominations who try to portray religion in a wealth of colors that dazzle the eye as a poetic arcadia, an easily attainable rung of simplicity, wholeness, and romantic tranquility, are, in actuality, bleeders of the very soul whose wounds they are promising to assuage. They are bleeders of the soul even if, scared as they often are of their own simplifications, they divide their sermons in inequal measure between depicting the terrors of hellfire and describing the utopian bliss that religion can bestow upon man.

This childish mixture of naivete and superficiality, of easy promises and fiery reprimands, is not confined to the pulpit or the TV screen. It is now refined in the furnace of a popular "philosophy" and "theology" and is transformed into a universal religious ideology. This ideology pretends to know and show the way to acquire a fine psychic equilibrium, pleasing to God and man, without toil, that is to say, without paying the price in spiritual agony and without undergoing a slow, gradual, painful process of transformation. The religionist how-toism, one might add, has now become part and parcel of an instant-satisfaction culture bursting with recipes for instant happiness, success, and mental cure-alls. There is not much difference between the "how to" of a Joyce Brothers, for example ("How to get everything you want out of life") and that of a Christian Scientist who believes that a person can acquire spiritual and physical healing in a single moment of "instant grace."

The Rav regards the saccharinic romantization of religion, on the one hand, and its utilitarian simplification, on the other, as equally destructive and deceptive. For religious consciousness to really matter in the life of man it cannot be anything but extraordinarily complex, rigorous, and often even tortuous. "The religious experience from beginning to end is antinomic and antithetic. It is a raging, clamorous torrent of man's consciousness" ("The Halakhic Man").

Such thoughts are, of course, unthinkable in Hasidic literature. No Hasidic master, except perhaps Rabbi Mendl of Kotzk, could have uttered such thoughts. Maybe that is why the great Kotzker did not hesitate at times to spoil the joy of a Hasidic *Farbrengen*. To state, as the Rav does, that where you find the complexity of religion, there you find its greatness, is to stress depth over ecstasy. But depth is something which is acquired through study much more than through prayer. Why, study *is* prayer, according to the sages, as is the case with the reciting of the Mishnah for the elevation of the souls of the departed. Hence the Rav's revealing assertion—and he is the first to make it so categorically—that it is the bet hamedrash, the house of study, and not the synagogue, that has played the leading role in Jewish life.

If existentialism is primarily interested in man, and religious existentialism, in man as created by the Creator to complete himself, that is to say, to complete creation, this interest is bound to express itself, above all, in an aversion to superficiality and deceptiveness, particularly religious superficiality and deceptiveness. On the one hand, it says no to the scientific image of man, but, on the other, it says no to the false spiritual comforters (or "spiritual leaders") who speak of faith and love as if these were easily acquirable commodities in some religious supermarket. It says no even to a religiosity which stresses prayer over study and ecstasy over depth. The Rav almost as a rule, is exceedingly careful not to say anything derogatory about Hasidism. Yet one cannot free oneself from the impression that the Rav sees the two hundred-year-old opposition of the Lithuanian Mitnagdim to Hasidim as having been clearly vindicated by the passing of time.

When the Rav continually refers to the homo religiosus as a mystic, it is quite obvious that he means the Hasid, but he refuses to spell this out, presumably for the sake of *shalom bayit*, even at the risk of presenting himself as a nonmystic. But the mysticism the Rav keeps his distance from is the easy supernaturalism and "spiritual drunkenness" that so often borders on escapism. The supernatural dimension one attains to through the study of the Torah, however—the Torah of which the Rav asserts that it actually proves God's existence—is attained by the exceedingly long and difficult road which leads to the mystical mating of commandment with mystery. The experience of this mating is distinctly supernatural and in this sense the Rav is undoubtedly a mystic. How else could he have embraced the Lurianic principle of *tzimtzum*, a cornerstone of kabbalistic mysticism, and turned it into the core of a dialectical edifice rising to the heights of a theonomy—not a theology but a theonomy—of pathos?

No, it is not mysticism which the Rav has reservations about, but *easy* mysticisms. The scarcity of true halakhic men versus the abundance of "mystics" among the Hasidim, the few outstanding *talmidei ḥakhamim* notwithstanding,[2] inevitably lends some weight to the old claim of the Lithuanian Mitnagdim that the Hasidic

---

2. The only Hasidic master of whom the Rav speaks with great admiration is Reb Shneor Zalman of Liadi, the founder of the Lithuanian Ḥabad movement. In *The Halakhic Man* he refers to him as to "that great luminary of Halakhah and mysticism" who sensed that "the fundamental method of the Halakhah is that act of quantification which is so integral a part of the mystery of the *tzimtzum*."

movement, indirectly, but unmistakably, spurned rabbinic learning. But there is also something else which seems to have induced the Rav to be wary of the otherworldliness of Hasidic teaching, and that is the impression among the majority of people, Jews and Gentiles alike, that a certain external appearance that can hardly be regarded as aesthetic, is supposed to attest to a particularly ardent form of Jewish religiosity.

If the Rav regards the halakhic man as superior to the homo religiosus it is not only because the former knows more, but because he *is* more—as a personality! To the three degrees of development, as defined by Kierkegaard, the aesthetic, the ethical, and the religious, the Rav adds what to him seems to be the highest—the halakhic. The halakhic contains the three other categories, that is why the halakhic man possesses personality. In contrast to homo religiosus, the Rav writes, "Halakhic man forges for himself a concrete, this-worldly personality. . . . The a priori law molds man's permanent character and imprints its stamp on his physiognomy. The countenance of the rabbinic scholar testifies to a strength of mind and a spiritual stature that sheds its brilliant light near and far. . . . His whole being is imbued with the dignity of uniqueness and individuality, and displays a distinct streak of aristocracy."

Unlike the homo religiosus, who stands and waits for the revelation of the truth and inspiration by the spirit, the Rav says, halakhic man does not look for "ecstatic paroxysms, frenzied experiences that whisper intimations of another world into his ears." He pays no attention to any "murmurings of intuition or other types of mysterious presentiments. . . . He is not particularly submissive and retiring and is not meek when it is a matter of maintaining his own views. Neither modesty nor humility characterizes the image of halakhic man. On the contrary, his most characteristic feature is strength of mind. . . . If he does battle for every jot and tittle of the Halakhah, he is motivated not only by a deep piety, but by a passionate love of truth. He recognizes no authority other than the authority of the intellect (obviously in accordance with the principles of tradition). He hates intellectual compromises or fence-straddling, intellectual flabbiness, and any type of wavering in matters of law and judgment."

This intellectual autonomy, which made it legitimate for some giants of the Halakhah to talk back, so to speak, to Heaven, by reminding the Supreme Legislator that the Torah, given to man, must be left to the autonomous domain of his intellect, bestows upon halakhic man the power not just to rule, but to reign, a power that grows as the esteem for him intensifies on account of his luminous personality. "In no other field of knowledge," the Rav says (in "The Halakhic Man"), "has man been adorned with the crown of absolute royalty as in the realm of Torah. The glorification of man reaches here the peak of splendor."

The outstanding halakhic men down the ages did not have to occupy any position of authority whatsoever in order to be universally recognized as the ultimate authorities on any question, let alone questions pertaining to halakhic matters, which Jewish communities anywhere in the world were preoccupied with. Once such a sage was discovered, and be it even in the remotest place, people from all over would flock to his side and feel privileged to weave crowns for his head. This is the power and the glory of the halakhic personality!

PERSONALITY AND HALAKHIC MAN

"That man who studies the Torah . . . Behold, how pleasant his ways, how accomplished his deeds! It is of him that the passage says: 'you are My servant, Israel, in whom I shall take pride' (Yoma 86:1)."

That is how halakhic man was seen down the ages: a person whom the Torah transformed into a *personality*.

The Rav, as we have seen, characterizes the halakhic man as a breed all by itself. The popular saying that the Shekhinah rests upon the true *talmid ḥakham* is no mere phrase. It has been regarded down the ages as a matter of verifiable truth. Even the physiognomy of the *talmid ḥakham* is affected by his nobleness: he radiates a light!

Not enough attention has been paid to the notion of light in Jewish tradition from biblical times on. Light seems to be not only a metaphor, but a substance. Moses descends Mount Sinai and his face radiates a light so dazzling that the Israelites are afraid to look at it. The giants of Halakhah down the ages were not only luminaries of the spirit but, yes *physically* luminous. Thus the sages of the Talmud do not hesitate to state that "A *talmid ḥakham* whose face does not glow like that of an angel of God disqualifies himself as a teacher of the Torah." Nothing in religious literature as a whole can be compared to the verification-test of the Shekhinah as a visible presence to which this astonishingly bold maxim invites!

But are we to assume that even with such a verification-test, as indeed, with the proof of God's existence, which, so the Rav assures us, is provided by the very study of the Torah *lishma*, all questions are answered and all doubts are vanquished? By no means! The Rav would not subscribe to the famous dictum of a Hasidic master that "to the nonbeliever there are no answers; to the believer there are no questions." In "Sacred and Profane" the Rav states that the modern representatives of religion are in error when they promise their followers a solution to all of life's problems—"an expectation which religion does not fulfill." Religion, the Rav asserts, "*deepens* the problem." He cites, as an example, the problem of theodicy, the justification of evil in the world, which has tantalized inquiring minds since time immemorial and is particularly provoked by the Shoah. This problem "has grown for the religious person in essence and dimensions." Thus, when a minister, a rabbi, or a priest attempts to solve the ancient problem of Job's suffering through a sermon or lecture, he does them a disservice. "The beauty of religion with its grandiose vistas reveals itself to men not in solutions, but in problems, not in harmony, but in the constant conflict of diversified forces and trends."

TZIMTZUM AS AN EXISTENTIAL EXPERIENCE

We have already mentioned that the Rav, who does not regard himself as a mystic, has embraced in toto the mystical notion, paradigmatic to Lurianic Kabbalah, of *tzimtzum*.

The Infinite would never reach out to the finite if the finite, i.e., man, did not possess the power to reach out to the Infinite. The finite, however, can try to reach out for the Infinite without possessing the power to become a receptacle of the Infinite. In other words, one cannot be a halakhic man without being a homo religiosus, but one can be a homo religiosus without being a halakhic man. To explain the process by which the Infinite "finitizes" itself, as it were, so as to become a partner in creativity with the Creator, the Rav resorts to the kabbalistic notion of *tzimtzum*.

Mysticism? The Rav does not regard himself as a mystic, though from time to time he lands on mystical heights, like the "Great Eagle" in whose footsteps he goes—and we mean, of course, Maimonides. Even when the Rav explains the difference between *tzimtzum* as understood by halakhic man and as perceived by kabbalists, there is an element of mysticism involved. Why is the "appearance of a mysterious transcendence in the midst of our concrete world," which, in the Rav's words, "the Halakhah denotes," any less of a mystical experience than the ascent into transcendence of the manifestly immanent? Be that as it may, here there appears to be only a difference between two mystical notions, or, if you will, directions: one dealing with transcendence, or ascent, the other with descent. That is how the Rav defines it (in "The Halakhic Man"): "While mysticism repairs the flaws of creation by 'raising it on high'; by returning it back to the source of pure, clear existence, the Halakhah fills the 'deficiency' by drawing the Shekhinah, the Divine Presence, downward, into the lowly world; by 'contracting' transcendence within our flawed world."

The theory of *tzimtzum*, or "contraction", is easily traceable to the Scripture and the sages, but it was defined with surpassing clarity of thought by the legendary Rabbi Yitzhak Luria, known as the Holy Ari. The essence of Lurianic thought is that in order for the Infinite, the Absolute Spirit, to create a material world, He had, as it were, to undergo a process of "withdrawal": the deliberate withdrawal of the Absolute Spirit, its "contraction," made it possible for a material world to emerge. As we shall see in the chapter on *teshuvah*, the Rav regards this Divine "withdrawal" as an example for repentant man to emulate in the spirit of Imitatio Dei. The mystery of *tzimtzum*, as the Rav sees it, is "the wondrous principle which expresses itself in two parallel dimensions: in the real world—in empirical reality, and in the ideal world—in halakhic constructions. The Supernal will clothes itself in these two creations and becomes embodied through them in the attribute of

strength (*gevurah*) and contraction." God has introduced a paral-
lelism in creativity: "The 'movement' from quality to quanity,
from experience to equations, which takes place in the real,
empirical world, also finds its expression in the ideal world of
Halakhah" ("The Halahic Man").

In the ideal world of Halakhah, the concept of holiness means
the descent of Divinity into our concrete world. That is how laws
dealing with the unmistakably quantifiable become building blocks
of the purely spiritual. The Rav (in "The Halakhic Man") quotes
the passage which says: "For the Lord thy God walketh in the
midst of thy camp. Therefore shall thy camp be holy" (Deut.
23:15) and explains: "It is the contraction of Infinity within a
finitude bound to laws, measures, and standards; the appearance
of transcendence within empirical reality."

This is, if one may say so, an existential transcendence. For in
the light of the ideal of creation and its issue, creativity, stored up
in the treasure house of Halakhah, "creation means the realization
of the idea of holiness. . . . The nothingness and naught, the
privation and the void are rooted in the realm of the profane. The
harmonious existence, the perfected being, are grounded in the
idea of the holy. If man wishes to attain the rank of holiness, he
must become a creator of worlds."[3]

Tzimtzum, as seen by the Rav, is the lowering of transcendence
into the midst of our turbid, coarse, material world. And this
lowering, which is the essence of creation as well as the peak of
creativity, can take place only through the implementation of the
ideal Halakhah in the core of reality.

---

1. In the Lithuanian Musar yeshivot, with whose founding fathers the Rav does not
always see eye-to-eye, this idea was basic. An illustrious Lithuanian *talmud hakham*,
Gedalyahu Alon, of blessed memory, had this to say on the subject: "As for the commandments, one rule applies to all commandments and to all good deeds. 'Any defector sparing
of oneself is a destruction of worlds'; 'Man's every deed is eternity.' " Of course, acute
tension ensues. "But it is countered by every shadow of a good thought in the mind and by
even the slightest manifestation of kindness, the central point of the creation of the world,
the source of man's nourishment." Such action is meritorious and a definite commandment.
The rabbis therefore listed, among the three commandments which Noahides observe, that,
though they eat it, they do not sell carrion in the marketplace and they do not write a
marriage certificate between two males (Hulin 92b).

HOLDING FAST TO THE EXISTING GOD

At this point, one cannot help but compare the religious existentialism of the Rav with some Buberian God ideas which are usually subsumed under "religious existentialism." Buber, as is well known, speaks of "the God we know as the personal one [whom] we experience in the immediacy of the dialogues."

Consequently, Buber states, man can find God only in the fullness of life and in the midst of the world by relating himself to God. On the other hand, he writes, the interpretation of God as becoming "visible" to man only in dialogue also makes possible an eclipse of God, etc. God, as Buber sees it, "lives only in the 'I-Thou' relation," which is true, of course. But whenever we come across this famous Buberism, we are somehow perplexed by the question of how man can conduct a "dialogue" with anyone—above all, God—without being given, or having accepted, some guidelines as to *how* to conduct such a dialogue. Buber, to be sure, does speak of such guidelines, and we should quote him verbatim. Seemingly referring to Kierkegaard's interpretation of the sacrifice of Isaac as of a "teleological suspension of the ethical," Buber writes (in "The Eclipse of God"): "It can happen [however] that a sinful man is uncertain whether he does not have to sacrifice his son to God for his sins (Micah 6:7). For Micah mutates the voice of God. In contrast to this, God Himself demands of this as of every man (not of Abraham, His chosen one, but of you and me) nothing more than justice and love, and that he 'walk humbly' with Him, with God (Micah 6:8)—in other words, not much more than the fundamental ethical."

To this Prof. Steven T. Katz rightly remarks (in "Hasidism and Modern Man"): "But given Buber's view of religious law and his rejection of the objective existence of that very 'Fundamental Ethical' to which he here appeals, it is logically impossible for him to maintain this line of defense. Micah can refer to the 'fundamental ethical' because he accepts the Torah as literally true and its ethical concepts as objective standards that are binding on all without question. Buber, by contrast, knows neither Torah as revealed contents nor ethical norms as objective prescriptions commanded by the Divine. . . . Certainly, man receives from all things and events a Divine claim on his person, but in general no indication is thereby given him as to what he should do for God in this hour, in this situation.''

Whether Buber realized it or not, his simplistic interpretation of Micah turns the God-man relationship into a one-way street and leaves no place whatsoever for the famous "I-Thou" in a God-man dialogue. If "no indication is given as to what he should do for God in this hour, in this situation," one is left, Buber's assertions notwithstanding, wondering how he can "hold on fast" to an "existing God" who has never deigned to tell man how this "holding fast" unto Him can be achieved. Using, as Buber does, a prophetic bottom line like Micah's famous lines—utterly unachievable as a practice without a life-long pursuit—has as much meaning as the carved letters of those same lines on a very fashionable temple in New York City, where anyone who knows anything about "walking humbly with thy God" would either be automatically disqualified as a member or would instinctively shun it as a prayer house.

THE LOWERING OF TRANSCENDENCE AS THE ONLY POSSIBLE "I-THOU"

What is left of the Divine-human "I-Thou" if, as Buber maintains, "what he [man] now grasps, concludes, decides from out of himself, this he draws out of his conscience"? ("Hasidism and Modern Man"). Nothing! Small wonder that Buber's popularity is greater among Christians than among Jews: his religiosity belongs to the area of "easy grace" which the German martyr priest Dietrich Bonhoeffer warned against as he held fast, in a concentration camp, to the "Old Testament"—much more "fast" it seems, than Buber's "holding on fast to the existing God."

THE HALAKHAH AS TESTIMONY TO THE PRESENCE OF THE DIVINE

There is no other way of "holding on fast to the existing God" but through the Torah. It has been said of Franz Rosenzweig by a colleague of his that he needed no theological theory "when life

itself, lived under the law, testified to the presence of the Divine''
(Nahum Glatzer). This is another way of expressing the Rav's
famous thought that ''the halakhic man does not need any proof
that God exists. The Torah proves it'' (''Halakhic Man'').

And it proves it not theologically—there is no theology in the
Torah!—but ontologically. Nowhere is the secret of *tzimtzum*, or
contraction, more manifest and relevant than in the minutest detail
of the law experienced as a true means of ''holding on fast to the
existing God.'' Only an insider can bear testimony to this connection between a so-called dry legalism and ''I am the Lord your
God.'' Rabbi Israel Salanter, the founder of the Lithuanian Musar
movement, spelled it out even more ''graphically'' when he said
that there is a connection between the study of a seemingly minute
detail of the law dealing, of all things, with ''an ox that gored a
cow'' and character improvement! (Of the mitzvot in general, the
sages say that their purpose is to refine man.)

No outsider, even a learned outsider, an outsider who knows
the Torah but does not believe in its Divine origin, will ever
understand how yeshiva boys could sit and sway as if in prayer
studying ecstatically a law concerning ''an ox that gored a cow''!
To the insider, however, it is crystal-clear that when the serious
Torah student emerges from an involved study of the ''dry legalism'' dealing even with ''an ox that gored a cow,'' he will be less
likely to transgress the law of ''honor thy father and thy mother.''
How can this be explained? The Rav, very careful, as mentioned,
to avoid easy mysticisms, provides the answer: *tzimtzum*. There is
a dialectical affinity between the infinitesimal and the infinite.
Transcendence is embodied in man's minutest deed. ''Every deed
is eternity.''

That is why the Rav puts so much emphasis on the paradigmatic
thought that holiness denotes the appearance of a mysterious
transcendence in the midst of our concrete world—that is to say,
the ''descent'' of God, whom no thought can grasp, onto Mount
Sinai; the bending down of a hidden and concealed world and
lowering it onto the face of reality.

The Rav transplants the mystical notion of *tzimtzum* into the
very heart of halakhic ontology. But before he does so, he defines
on more than one occasion the difference between the two: in
mystical doctrine, the idea of the *tzimtzum*, or contraction, of the

Divinity, so as to make it possible for a physico-material world to emerge, inevitably touches upon questions of cosmogony. "Unlike the kabbalists," the Rav states with a boldness that may require some clarification, "and (mutatis mutandis) Philo, Plotinus, the Neoplatonists and the Renaissance philosophers, the Halakhah does not concern itself with metaphysical mysteries" ("The Halakhic Man")." Since the law of Halakhah is a practical-utilitarian one, one should not compare the concept of *tzimtzum* in the Halakhah with the concept as it appears in mystical doctrine. To the Rav, one should add, the passage "And let them make Me a sanctuary that I shall dwell among them" (Exodus 25:8)—Almighty God whose glory fills the earth, "contracting himself, as it were, in His sanctuary—prefigures the notion of *tzimzum*, though hardly as perceived in subsequent mystical interpretations."

Mystical doctrine expounds a metaphysical system that penetrates into the hidden recesses of creation, being and nothingness, the beginning and the end. In the Halakhah, however, "the concept of *tzimtzum* does not pertain to the secrets of creation and the chariots, but rather to law and judgment. Therefore the halakhic man's ontological outlook differs radically from the mystic's."

The mystic, in the Rav's definition, sees the world as a kind of affront, heaven forbid, to God's glory. That is why the desire of mystical doctrine is to free both man and the Shekhinah, the Divine Presence, from the world and from the visible reality which is imprinted with the stamp of the supernal. Halakhic man, by contradiction, does not chafe against existence. He does not wish to free himself from the world. He is completely suffused with an unqualified ontological optimism that is totally immersed in existence. The task of man, as seen by the Halakhic Man, "is to bring down the Divine Presence to the lower world, to this vale of tears. . . . The mystery of *tzimtzum* should not precipitate metaphysical anguish, but rather gladness and joy. Man resides together with his Creator in this world, and it is only through cultivating this togetherness in the here and now that man can acquire a share in the world-to-come" ("The Halakhic Man").

It is in this spirit of halakhic *tzimtzum* that one can understand as mentioned, what the sages of the Talmud meant when they said: "All that the Holy One has got in the world are the four cubits of the law." Without the dialectics of *tzimtzum* this thought would have been seen by the outsider as the epitome of narrow-minded-ness. The dialectics of *tzimtzum*, however, raises it to the level of holiness where precisely the preoccupation with the infinitesimal may qualify us as recepticles of the Infinite!

HALAKHIC MAN AND THE MATHEMATICIAN

The Rav finds a striking resemblance between halakhic man and the mathematician, who masters infinity for the sake of creating finitude, delimited by numbers and mathematical measures, and cognizing it. The Halakhah, from the perspective of the process of contraction, also uses the method of quantification: it quantifies quality and religious subjectivity in the form of concrete, objective phenomena that are standardized and measurable. "The laws relating to standards, interpositions, and partitions, are laws re-vealed to Moses on Mount Sinai" (Eruvin 4a, Sukkah 5b). Here Sinaic quality is clearly subjected to *tzimtzum*, or contraction, by means of quantification. The Rav goes even further, maintaining that Galileo's statement that "the great book that ever lies before our eyes—the universe—is written in mathematical language and the characters are triangles, circles, and other geometrical fig-ures," applies as well to the Halakhah. The fundamental tendency of the Halakhah is to translate the qualitative features or religious subjectivity—the contents of religious man's consciousness—which surges and swells like the waves of the sea, then pounds against the shores of reality, where they shatter and break—into firm and well-established quantities, "like nails well fastened that no storm can uproot them from their place" (Eccles. 12:11). The Supernal will is thus reflected both in the mirror of reality and the mirror of ideal Halakhah through the medium of objective, quanti-tative measurements.

The Rav's insistence on halakhic *experience* as objectivity requires clarification. All existentialist philosophers, starting with Kierkegaard, stress the truth of subjectivity as opposed to "objec-tivization." Kierkegaard states that "truth *is* subjectivity." In opposition, Hegel and the idealist-philosophers propounded the idea of a "universal spirit" revealing itself in history and unmindful of the individual. Men like Kierkegaard and later Dostoyevsky, rose in protest against the "objectivity" of, as an example, "commonly held truths." The Rav, in contradiction, states that "experience has shown that the whole religious ideology which bases itself on the subjective nature of religion—from Schleiermacher, to Kant, to Natrop—can have dangerous, destructive consequences that far outweigh any putative gains" ("The Halakhic Man").

How are we to understand this apparent contradiction? The answer, in the view of this author, can be only one: Truth is subjectivity from the angle of *receiving*, but from the angle of the *perceived imparting*—and we are dealing here, after all, with God as the *imparter*—it is pure objectivity. When Kant, whom we shall discuss in another chapter, rejects Judaism on account of its submission to "statutes" imposed from "without," i.e., the law, the "without" he rejects is precisely the normative, a priori objectivity we are talking about. The Divine "without," which is pure objectivity, becomes a supreme subjective experience in the halakhic man.

WHEN THE SUBJECT MATTER CHANGES INTO INNER POWER

"Teaching begins," Franz Rosenzweig writes, "when the subject matter ceases to be subject matter and changes into inner power" ("The Builders").

The Rav relates an extraordinary episode that dramatizes the truth of this existential maxim, though with one little change: The point at which subject matter ceases to be subject matter and changes into inner power is not exactly where teaching begins, but where it *culminates*. The Rav's example certainly points in that direction, for it deals with a major subject matter called fear of death exposed to the inner power of a master of the Halakhah. "When death becomes an object of man's cognition," the Rav asserts, "the fright accompanying death dissipates." In other words, "when man succeeds in transforming death-subject into death-object, the horror is gone." How is this achieved? The Rav's father, himself a *talmid ḥakham* of the first order, related to the Rav that when the fear of death took hold of Reb Haim, the Rav's luminous grandfather, he would throw himself, heart and mind,

into the study of the laws of "tents and . . . corpse defilement"!
Immersion in the intricate minutiae of the Torah laws concerning
such different and complex problems as the defilement of a grave
or a tent, blocked-up defilement, interposition before defilement, a
vessel with a tight-fitting cover upon it in a tent in which a corpse
lies, etc., would assuage Reb Haim's fear of death, calm the
turbulence of his soul, and "imbue him with a spirit of joy and
gladness." The Rav's explanation? "The act of objectification
triumphed over the subjective fear of death" ("The Halakhic
Man").

The question, of course, arises: Can this case be regarded as
typical of halakhic man's ability to counter the fear of death, or
does it illustrate that it takes an extraordinary halakhic man like
Reb Haim to perform such a feat? I shall not try to answer this
question. It appears, however, that the Rav's notions of objectivity
and subjectivity are not always clearly defined. For is it not true
that while the Torah is the epitome of objectivity, the *talmid
hakham* experiences it, on the summit of his knowledge, as an
overwhelmingly subjective sensation? Anyway, one thing clearly
emerges from the Rav's words: Reb Haim's treatment of the
subject of death is undoubtedly the highest expression of a mysterious dynamic inherent in the dialectics of Halakhah. Franz Rosenzweig knew exactly how to put it: "It robs death of its sting and
Hades of its pestilential smell" (*The Star of Redemption*).

BONDAGE TO THE HOLY ONE

But there is something else that comes to mind as we contemplate
the power of the halakhot dealing with death to mitigate the fear of
death: the psychological factor. The Rav refers to it in connection
with another situation, "bondage to the Holy One." Dr. Viktor
Frankl, the well-known existential psychotherapist, uses the term
"paradoxical intention" for a form of therapy in which the patient
is advised to deliberately face what he most fears.

The Rav relates a remark which was once made to him by an
eminent psychiatrist concerning the prayer recited on the High
Holy Days: "Cast Thy fear, O Lord . . ." If he had the authority
to do so, the psychiatrist told the Rav, he would have eliminated

this prayer from the prayer book, for fear is the major cause of the mental illnesses that beset mankind. In order to preserve one's mental health, the psychiatrist argued, one should be free of fear, and thus one should certainly not pray for fear.

The Rav, in reply, told the psychiatrist that fear seems to be a universal malaise. Some are afraid that they may not be able to succeed in their careers, others fear losing their wealth or their status, or that they will fail to attain sufficient prominence. Many people are afraid of sicknesses and bodily weakness. In generations past, the fear of leprosy engulfed the world; today people live in fear of cancerous growths—many people do not go to see a doctor even when they have pains lest he diagnose "the disease." Man is constantly plagued by all sorts of lesser fears. One major source of fear, however, the Rav went on, can wipe out all these lesser fears. One does not have to be a psychiatrist to know that. But, the Rav asked, what kind of fear is it that can overtake man, thereby uprooting all other kinds of fears—fears of failure, of poverty, of loneliness, of rejection, of old age, or of disease? *Only* the fear of the Lord! That, the Rav said, is the reason behind the expression in the High Holy Day prayers, "Cast Thy fear, O Lord, upon all Thy handiwork, and Thine awe upon all that Thou hast created." We pray, the Rav concluded, that this great fear will free us from all the lesser fears which lurk everywhere, upsetting and embittering our lives.

But we should not let go of the prayer that so upset the psychiatrist without an additional comment on the second part of the passage, which deals with awe. The first deals with fear (*pahad*), the second with awe (*emah*). Even a scant familiarity with the Rav's concept of *teshuvah* (repentance), of which we shall have more to say in another chapter, is enough to make one realize that it is awe of majesty, superseding even fear, which pervades the whole personality—and should pervade the personality of the true *ba'al teshuvah* in his relationship with God. *Emah* (awe) is seemingly a much higher rung than fear, and—which is even more important—a much higher rung even than love! Dostoyevsky, a devout Christian, has provided some astonishing insights into Christian fallacies (as in "The Grand Inquisitor"), but a detail in one of his novels speaks volumes about the irrelevance of Christian love when *awe* of Majesty is missing. Dostoyevsky tells the story of a poor peasant who finds himself one night in an inn next to a sleeping man, fully dressed, with a golden vest-watch scintillating over his belly. The desire to own that watch was so irresistible that he decided to inherit it by murder. He crossed himself, raised his head toward heaven muttering "Forgive me God for Christ's sake," and drew his knife. Dostoyevsky does not tell us the moral of the story, but we should not hesitate to draw it from its very source: the peasant *loved* God, but no, he did not fear Him. And even if he feared Him at times, as a father, he never knew the awe accorded to a king.

But coming back to the "bondage to the fear of God," as the Rav calls it, the peasant in the Dostoyevsky story knew nothing of bondage, nothing of fear as a deterrent—the kind of fear which frees one from other lower fears. Isn't it possible, one is tempted to ask, that the total subjective involvement in the hallowed halakhic objectivity of the law—even the law concerning death and dying—may free one of the terror of having lived in vain? Thus cognitive not-having-lived-in-vain may indeed "rob death of the sting and Hades of its pestilential smell" (Rosenzweig). It was said of the luminous Lithuanian *talmid hakham* and Musarnik, Rabbi Nahum Zvi Ziv, son of Rabbi Simha Zisl Broide of Kelm—and it was none other than his German doctor who said it, in Koenigsberg, where the great man died—that it was worthwhile to travel hundreds of miles just to see how Rabbi Nahum Zvi died.

TIME AND TIMELESSNESS OF THE HALAKHIC MAN

People, in their boredom, speak of the need "to kill time." To the halakhic man, however, it is the very opposite: The need to revive time by means of an authentic existence. There was a saying among Lithuanian *talmidei hakhamim*: "Don't dismiss the pleasures of this world: study Torah." Time is not there to be killed, but to be brought to life by a ceaseless dialogic relationship with personages of the Torah from eternity to here. To say, as Buber does, that man can "find God only in the fullness of life and in the midst of the world by relating himself to God" is an abstraction if the law is excluded. One cannot relate oneself to God without relating oneself to the bearers of His word down the ages. Thus the Halakhah, never losing sight of the tension between time and timelessness in halakhic interpretations, never loses sight of the creative continuity of generations of Torah scholars, who, across the ages, hold out their hearts and minds to each other.

This is the grand dialogue which halakhic men conduct with each other as if the participants in the dialogue were alive and present at the discussion. Thus the Rav speaks of "the Jewish people's outlook regarding the beautiful and resplendent phenomenon of time. . . . Time in this conception is not destructive, all-consuming, and it does not simply consist of fleeting, imperceptible moments. . . . there is a wonderful chain which originated in the bright morning of the day of revelation and stretches forward toward the eschaton. It represents the manner in which the Jewish people experience their own history in learning a history that floats upon the stormy waters of time. The consciousness of halakhic man, that master of the received tradition, embraces the entire company of the Mesorah. He lives in their midst, discusses and argues questions of Halakhah with them, delves into and analyzes fundamental halakhic principles in their company. All of them merge into one time experience. He walks alongside Maimonides, listens to Rabbi Akiba, senses the presence of Abaye and Raba. He rejoices with them and shares their sorrow. . . . There can be no death and no expiration among the company of the sages of tradition. Eternity and immortality reign here in unbounded fashion. Both past and future become, in such circumstances, ever-present realities" ("The Halakhic Man").

HE SENSES THE PRESENCE OF ABAYE AND RABA

Whoever has studied Torah in his youth has not only sensed the presence of Abaye and Raba while studying them in the yeshiva; Abaye and Raba became an endearing presence to him at home, in the street, and in his inner self for many years to come. We have here, of course, a blurring of the boundaries dividing time from eternity. But there is something else here, too: a blurring, as it were, of the boundaries between the Creator and His creatures. If "the most fervent desire of halakhic man is to behold the replenishment of the deficiency in creation," as the Rav puts it, a deficiency which was purposely left by the Perfect One for man to repair—man is here, after all, to complete creation!—then we understand why "the Holy One, blessed be He, rejoices in the dialectics of the Torah" (a popular folk-saying quoted by the Rav). We also understand something else, however; we namely understand how it came to pass that *talmidei hakhamim* and *tzadikim* down the ages were always described by contemporaries as projecting presences which could not have been so manifestly luminous if they, the contemporaries, were not conscious of the presence of a higher Presence. Thus, the Rav quotes Rabbi Haim of Volozhin, the most distinguished disciple of the Gaon of Vilna, who said that "when a person exerts himself to understand a halakhic matter clearly, then it is certain that the Shekhinah, the Divine Presence, rests upon him at the very moment of his studying, as the sages have said, 'God has in His world only the four cubits of Halakhah.' "

TZIMTZUM AS THE FOUR CUBITS OF HALAKHAH

It is, of course, as aforementioned, easy for neophytes to point at this talmudic adage as attesting to "narrow-mindedness." But the truth of the matter is that there is nothing more narrow-minded than the inability to see the seeming narrowness of the *min hametzar*, the "straits," as leading up to *merhavyah*, the "wide places," and, conversely, the impossibility that the so-called "wide places" could ever be initially conducive to man's calling upon God. This is something that can happen only from *min hametzar*. Authentic existence starts with an apprehension of *tzimtzum*, that is to say, *min hametzar*, "narrow straits", that lead to *merhavyah*!

The perception of the Halakhah as the *tzimtzum*, or contraction, of the Divine "within the four cubits of the law"—a thought which no outsider will ever understand—clearly sees the Shekhinah as a *presence*, as it is written, "And I have set the Lord before me always." The proverbial expression "The Shekhinah rests upon him"—a description of the halakhic man as seen down the ages even by simple people around him—is no impressionistic hyperbole. Nor is the experience of the *talmid ḥakham* himself in his encounter with a higher presence. In one of his not infrequent moments of moving frankness, the Rav declares: "Believe me when I tell you that I myself could have never endured the [trials and tribulations of his] past years had I not felt the close proximity of God. . . . I am not a Kabbalist nor a mystic, so when I speak of the nearness of God it is something I feel when opening the pages of the Talmud in order to study. When I am thus immersed in study, I feel as if the Almighty is there standing behind me, putting His hand on my shoulder, looking with me at the text lying on the table and asking me about it. This is not something I imagine. To me it is a true-to-life experience" ("The Halakhic Man").

We are dealing here, in other words, with the presence of a Presence. This presence, we should add, was also a true-to-life experience of the *talmidei hakhamim* from Sura and Pumpadita to the Eastern European shtetls, who always regarded the moments of *lernen* (which must not be confused with "learning"), in private or in groups, at home or in the house of study, as the experience of a presence that would serve, as an inner shield against their troubles, and, at the same time, as a source of protective light and joy under the most appalling circumstances. Rabbi Yehudah Halevi goes so far as to state (in the *Kuzari*) that "the Divine law confers something in the nature of angels on the human mind, something that cannot be acquired otherwise." The *Kuzari* quotes the *Book of Creation*, where the following is said of those who study the Torah: "Wherever some few, or a full community, are sufficiently pure, the Divine light rests upon them in an incomprehensible and miraculous manner which is quite outside the ordinary course of the natural world."

The Rav's perception of the Halakhah as the *tzimtzum* of the Shekhinah "within the four cubits of the law" thus clearly postulates the Shekhinah as a "presence." In the cases of some giants of the Halakhah down the ages, it was said by contemporaries, as in Rashi's case, that the Shekhinah was often present in his house of study. The proverbial expression "the Shekhinah rests on his face" summarized the popular impression of the man whose "whole being is imbued with the dignity of uniqueness and individuality, and displays a distinct streak of aristocracy," the Rav's characterization of the *talmid hakham* ("The Halakhic Man"). The very presence of a *talmid hakham* meant inspiration, light, and reassurance in Judaism. Hence the passage in Proverbs, "And thine eyes should *see* thy teachers."

But there is also a kind of objective presence which is known only to Halakhic Judaism: The Torah as a literally *living* presence. It is a matter of fact that the sages at times treated portions of the Torah as if they were actually alive. Thus Rabbi Shimon ben Yochai, alluding to the fact that the portion of "Judgments" in Exodus precedes all others dealing with the law, asks "Why did 'Judgments' *see fit* to precede all other mitzvot of the Torah?" The portion of the Torah is here endowed, as it were, with sight: "See fit"! By the same token, Rabbi Yosef Karo, the author of the *Shulhan Aruch*, speaks of the voice of the Mishnah which has spoken to him in his vision like a living being. Little attention has been paid to the manner in which a Torah scholar would refer to another whose knowledge he held in high esteem: "*Er ken lernen.*" Literally translated this means, "He knows knowing." Implied in this expression is, above all, the idea of the effort that goes into knowing: one has to know knowing. Knowing alone is not enough; one has to know knowing as one has to know him whom one really wants to know. The Rav describes this state most dramatically in the aforementioned passages where he refers, as to a "true-to-life experience," to the sensation of knowing as a Presence: "When I am thus immersed in study, I feel as if the Almighty is there, standing behind me, putting His hand on my shoulder, looking with me at the text lying on the table and asking me about it."

THE PROSE AND POETRY OF THE HALAKHAH

The sensation of knowing as a Presence is the poetic dimension of Halakhah—a dimension which the Rav rarely elaborates on without resorting to its seemingly "prosaic" realm. Thus halakhic man, to the Rav, "resembles somewhat the mathematician who masters infinity only for the sake of creating finitude." What follows is that halakhic man's relationship to existence is not only ontological, but normative in nature. In truth, the Rav avers, the ontological approach serves as the vestibule whence he may enter the banquet hall of normative understanding. There is an interplay going on all the time in the halakhic mind between the natural and the supernatural. Halakhic man cognizes the world in order to subordinate—and at the same time elevate—it to the rung of religious performances. He cognizes space by means of a religious a priori, lawful categories in order to realize in it, as an example, the halakhic norm of Sabbath, the commandment of sukkah, and the idea of purity. The halakhic man sometimes engages in the same kind of calculations as an astronomer, a point which Maimonides elaborated on in his "Laws of the Sanctification of the New Moon." He studies the plant world in order to classify their species, as such classification relates to the laws of diverse seeds, and for the purpose of determining standards of growth. Such determination, in turn, affects the agricultural laws.

As the Rav enumerates all these "prosaic" laws, the question arises again, How does the poetry of Halakhah grow out of such "legalisms"?

The Rav explains: "The halakhic man received the Torah from Sinai not as a simple recipient, but as a creator of worlds, as a partner of the Almighty in the act of creation. [It thus follows that] the power of creative interpretation—*hiddush*—is the very foundation of the received tradition" ("The Halakhic Man").

The key word is *hiddush*. One often wonders why it is that all the great thoughts expressed by the classics rarely if ever come through to their readers. But the reason may very well be that the written insights of others, no matter how great, are, at best, finely finished products which one may quote and admire, but rarely live by. To live by a great thought is to arrive at it oneself by means of a *hiddush*. The *hiddush* may be of a normative, legal, "objective" nature, but so great is the power of a *hiddush* in Torah that it refines and elates one's soul as it strains one's mind to the maximum. A *hiddush*, moreover, no matter what subject, adds purpose and certainty to life. That is what the Rav means when he speaks of "the power of creative interpretation as the very foundation of the received tradition." Any new *hiddush*, new insight in the Torah, even insights regarding standards and measurements, is endowed, at its peak, with creative joy and poetic vigor, and is part of the hoped-for subjective process of cleaving unto Him. It is not in vain, after all, that in Judaism—and in Judaism alone—study is prayer, and that the Mishnah, as aforementioned, is studied on Yahrtzeits for the souls of the departed as a matter of sacred tradition. That is why the Rav does not show much patience with mystical shortcuts to higher realms which miss the dialectical element of the halakhic *ḥiddush* as experienced by the *talmid hakham*. He, too, is ultimately—but *only* ultimately—led to the "cosmos," but via "simple acts of quantification which are so integral a part of the mystery of the *tzimtzum*" ("The Halakhic Man").

The poetry of the Halakhah emanates from what seems clearly prosaic, exactly as its timelessness often bursts forth from what is so manifestly "dated." Franz Rosenzweig understood this perfectly well when he interpreted the words "And eternal life He planted in our midst" to signify a destiny which, like the Torah, transcends the limits of historical time. But such a state of supreme awareness, according to the Rav, can be achieved only when "cognition precedes rapture." So suspicious is the Rav of easy raptures and facile mysticisms that he states without hesitation that "he who reaches a peak of enthusiasm prior to his having *cognized*, prior to his having completed his study, it is as if he has committed a moral sin."

And there is a yardstick by which degrees of cognition can be tested. The yardstick consists of the rung at which the Halakhah is experienced as being the realization of revelation in the realm of concrete life. On this level of cognition, it is also perceived as a vivid manifestation of timelessness within time. "Time is measured by the student of our Torah, which begins with creation of heaven and earth. Similarly, the halakhic man's future does not terminate with the end of his own individual future at the moment of death, but extends into the future of the people, the people who yearns for the coming of the Messiah and the Kingdom of God" ("The Halakhic Man").

The Rav, to illustrate the element of timelessness involved in the study of the Torah, stresses the fact that not only his father and grandfather, but other great *talmidei ḥakhamim* down the ages, would derive as much creative joy from gaining new insights into laws pertaining, as an example, to Temple sacrifices millennia ago, as to laws dealing with distinctly contemporary problems! It was due only to this extraordinary blending of the timely and the timeless that halakhic man, undergoing a process of ever more cognitive refinement or refining cognition, glowed, in the Rav's words, with a resplendent ethical beauty.[4]

---

4. "Space does not permit me," the Rav states at the conclusion of the first part of

THE ETERNALLY CONTEMPORARY

We were on the subject of the prose and poetry of the Halakhah as being on the same level as the halakhic treatment of time and timelessness.

An extraordinary example of the poetry of Halakhah as dialectically related to, and emerging from, its prose is provided by Prof. Isadore Twersky of Harvard. A son-in-law of the Rav, he is also, as could be expected, a halakhic man of the first magnitude and, at the same time, a philosopher—and a philosopher of Halakhah.

In *"Shulhan Arukh": The Enduring Code of Jewish Law*, Prof. Twersky was seemingly compelled, if that is the word for it, to tackle the enigma of "dry legalisms" assuming, as they do in the dialectics of the Halakhah, the *experiential* nature of what Max Scheller referred to as "the methodology of sanctification."

Prof. Twersky tried to explain the extraordinary dialectical relationship between the seemingly "dry" Halakhah and its ultimate ontological poesy by discussing the unique phenomenon of Rabbi Yosef Karo, brother-in-law of the Holy Ari of Safed, and author of the *Shulḥan Arukh*. Rabbi Yosef Karo was, in Prof. Twersky's words, an "arch-halakhist" and an "arch-kabbalist" at the same time. He was, without doubt, an arch-halakhist in the strictest sense of the word and is regarded as such to this day. Prof. Twersky writes: "The single, most important feature of the *Shulhan Arukh* is its unswerving concentration of prescribed patterns of behavior to the exclusion of any significant amount of theoretical data. The *Shulhan Arukh* is a manual for practical guidance, not academic study. . . . [moreover] unlike the *Mishneh*

"The Halakhic Man," "even to begin to speak, for example, about Reb Haim's unrelenting efforts to realize the ideals of righteousness and equity. Let me merely cite one incident wherewith to conclude this section. Once, two Jews died in Brisk on the same day. In the morning, a poor shoemaker who had lived out his life in obscurity died, while about noontime a wealthy, prominent member of the community passed away. According to the Halakhah, in such a case the one who dies first must be buried first. However, the members of the burial society, who had received a handsome sum from the heirs of the wealthy man, decided to attend to him first, for who was there to plead the cause of the poor man? When Reb Haim was informed about the incident, he sent a message of the court to warn the members of the burial society to desist from their disgraceful behavior. When the members of the society refused to heed the Rav's warning, Reb Haim arose, took his walking stick, trudged over to the house of the deceased, and chased all the attendants outside."

Torah [of Maimonides], or the *Turim* [of Rabbenu Asher] [it] does not abound in extra-halakhic comments, guiding tenets, and ideological directions. While the *Mishneh Torah* does reveal the full intellectualistic posture of Maimonides, the *Shulḥan Arukh* does not even afford an oblique glimpse of the kabbalistic posture of Rabbi Yosef Karo, who appears here in the guise of the civil lawyer for whom 'nothing was more pointless, nothing more inept than a law with a preamble.' "

"However," Prof. Twersky adds, "when all is said it would be incorrect and insensitive to assert unqualifiedly that the *Shulḥan Arukh*—that embodiment of Halakhah which Jewish history proclaimed supreme—is a spiritless, formalistic, even timid work." To dramatize this point, Prof. Twersky quotes the opening sentence of the *Shulḥan Arukh* as elaborated by Rabbi Moshe Iserles (the Ramo), who characterized it as "the nerve center of the entire halakhic system and the fountain of its strength."

The cardinal principle of the Torah and the noble path of the righteous is epitomized in the words of the Psalms, "I have set the Lord always before me." Prof. Twersky quotes the Ramo's elucidation of this passage. "Man," says the Ramo, "does not act, move, and occupy himself when he is alone in the house as when he sits, moves, and occupies himself in the presence of a great king." To be in the presence of a great king, one might add, is not only to know what to say and how to say it, but what to wear, how to look, and even how to tie one's shoelaces. To miss any detail would bear testimony to a lack of preparedness. Such a lack is tantamount to a vacuum.

HALAKHAH ABHORS A VACUUM

"Halakhah, like nature," Prof. Twersky avers, "abhors a vacuum." This statement points simultaneously in two opposite directions: the direction of a pursuit which abhors vacuums, and of another which, willy-nilly, breeds them. We know by now that ingenuity, having outrun intelligence, has become a mass producer of vacuums. We know, moreover, that excesses of freedom, freedoms taken in excess, breed anomie, a state of feelinglessness which, according to Dr. Rollo May, has now assumed epidemic proportions. Those who seek an escape from the vacuum in what people call "happiness" are increasingly aware of how vacuous that happiness can be if it leaves the soul out of the equation. But the soul, like the Halakhah, abhors vacuums! At the present stage of history, when it appears increasingly clear that freedom has failed to rescue man from the bondage of nothingness, it seems as if the universal Lawgiver, foreseeing a time when misused freedom would be as debasing as, say, chains, created "chains"—normative chains—which will secure true freedom. "Don't read *harut*," the sages say, "engraved on the tablets of the law," but "*herut* [Freedom]." The law *is* freedom.

Such a freedom, in Prof. Twersky's words, recognizes no twilight zone of neutrality and futility, and is all-inclusive. Consequently, every action, even the tying of one's shoelaces, can be and is invested with symbolic meaning. "Nothing is accidental, behavioral, purely biological. Even unavoidable routine is made less perfunctory." "Halakhah . . . is a tense, vibrant, dialectical system which regularly insists upon normativeness in action and inwardness in feeling and thought. It undertook to give continuous expression to theological ideas, ethical norms, ecstatic moods and historical concepts, but never superseded or eliminated these ideals or concepts. Halakhah itself is therefore a coincidence of opposites: prophecy and law, charisma and institution, mood and medium, image and reality, the thought of eternity and the life of temporality."

"The thought of eternity and the life of temporality." As I came across those lines, I was reminded of the truly beautiful manner in which a great French poet and thinker, Paul Valéry, defined the sage: "He didn't consult the old in him, for he himself was old; he didn't consult the new in him, for he himself was new: he consulted in himself the eternally contemporary."

It is the Halakhah as the eternally contemporary, or, as Prof. Twersky puts it, "the thought of eternity and the life of temporality," which in the Rav's thought, too, turns subject matter into a source of inner power. It is not in vain that halakhic Jews seek this power not only in order to know but in order to live. Thus Ludwig Lewisohn, in his *What Is the Jewish Heritage?*, repeats a story about a small group of Jewish survivors of the Nazi Holocaust who were making their way, in 1946, from their Siberian exile westwards to the Polish shtetl that had once been their home.

"The town was a mass of rubble. They did not find even graves. All their kith and kin had been burned in the crematoriums. The synagogue was in ruins, but a stair to the cellar had been saved. Descending that stair, these Jews found a few talmudic volumes, charred and water-soaked, but still usable in part. They procured them a few tallow-candles and sat down to read a page or two. There came one running then and cried: 'Jews, did you forget that you are running for your lives? The Soviets are closing the frontiers. The American zone is still far off. Flee!' And one of the group waved the messenger aside; 'Shah!' he said gravely, ('Be still!') *'M'darf lernen!'* ('One must learn!')."

2

Confrontation

CONFRONTED MAN AND AUTHENTIC EXISTENCE

The Rav introduced the term "confrontation" into existentialist thought: only *confronted* man can lay claim to what is usually referred to in existential philosophy as "authentic existence."

Clearly, there is in the Rav's thought a wealth of existentialist themes. To mention just a few: the disregard for the "in general" as against the actually lived; the aversion to the easy, commonly held "truths" as against the cognitive experience of creativity as growth; the accent on life as drama, tension, and struggle as against the predictability of a mechanical existence in conformity with the life order; the insistence on man's awesome responsibility going hand-in-hand with his capability to generate new laws of causation as against the terribly misused deterministic freedoms, often bordering on the animalistic ("Divine image or a beast of prey"); the strong sense of human involvement in this world and the call for authenticity of existence—confrontation—as opposed to the ejection of man into the thoughtless exterior; and the rejection of the nonreflective, uniform, unperturbed life as opposed to the vital tension inherent in the quest for authentic existence as a process permeated by the dialectical dynamics of becoming.

To fully understand the Rav's notion of confrontation, as elaborated in his essay of the same name, we should resort to one of his lucid ontologic-homiletical interpretations of a biblical narrative which deals with confrontation in both the literal and the figurative sense (Gen. 32: 18–20). Patriarch Jacob, in his instructions to his agents, prior to his much-feared confrontation with his alienated brother Esau, tells them as follows: "When Esau, my brother,

35

meeteth thee and asketh thee, saying: Whose are thou, and whither goest thou, and whose are these before thee?'' etc. The Rav reads this passage as containing questions which go way beyond the obvious: "My brother Esau will address to you three questions: 'Whose art thou?'—To whom do you, as a metaphysical being, as a soul, as a spiritual personality, belong?; 'And whither goest thou?'—To whom is your historical destiny committed? To whom have you consecrated your future? What is your ultimate goal, your final objective? Who is your God, and what is your way of life?' These inquiries are related to your identity as members of a convenantal community. However,'' Jacob continued, "my brother Esau will also ask another question: 'And whose are these before thee?'—Are you ready to consecrate your talents, capabilities, and efforts toward the material and cultural welfare of general society?''

As regards the last question, the Rav extrapolates, "Jacob told his agents to answer in the affirmative. 'It is a present unto my lord, even unto Esau.' Yes, we are determined to participate in every civic, scientific, and cultural enterprise. We feel obligated to enrich society with our creative talents and to be constructive and useful citizens. But as far as the other questions are concerned— 'Whose are thou? And whither goest thou?'—Jacob commanded his agents to reply in the negative. He commanded them most categorically to tell Esau that their souls, their personalities, their metaphysical destinies belong exclusively to God, and His servant Jacob; 'They are thy servant Jacob's,' and no human power can succeed in severing the bond between them and the God of Jacob.''

The idea of confrontation in this biblical narrative is prefigured on various levels: the physical, the metaphysical, the general, and the Jewish. It is also prefigured on the level—or against the background—of fear and trembling: "And Jacob was greatly afraid and distressed'' (Gen. 32:7).

This, according to the Rav, is the uniquely Jewish mode of confrontation, or, more exactly, of *double* confrontation. If the alienated Jewish intellectual is doubly alienated, as he so often is, alas—alienated as a Jew and as an intellectual—a truly authentic Jew confronts the threat of alienation with the spiritual armor of the covenantal faith community. It is a uniquely Jewish confrontation, though not a uniquely Jewish challenge, for the existential challenge itself issues from a built-in and Divinely willed dichotomy in human nature. It is not in vain, as we are taught by the sages, that the biblical word *vayitzer* ("created"), when applied to man—not to animals but to man—is spelled in the Torah, where every letter counts, with two yods, *vayyitzer*, signifying the two *yetzers* ("urges") with which man was originally created.

And indeed the dichotomy in human nature—we may as well call it duality—is as old as man. This dichotomy, anchored not in original sin, but in an original plan of the Creator's, explains, according to the Rav's interpretation, the seemingly inexplicable fact that the Bible presents us with two different versions of the creation of man. In the Rav's juxtaposition of the two Adams, either as two different aspects of the same Adam or as two different types of man, we distinguish three progressive levels. The first is described in Genesis 2:5–7 and reads as follows: "And every plant of the field was not yet in the earth, and every herb of the field had not yet grown. . . . And there was no man to till the ground. But there went up a mist from the earth and watered the whole face of the ground. And the Lord God formed man from the dust of the ground and breathed into his nostrils the breath of life and man became a living soul."

We deal here, in the Rav's interpretation, with the *Urmensch* determined by biological immediacy and mechanical necessity. He knows no responsibility, no opposition, no dichotomy and no fear. He is free from carrying the load of humanity and there is nothing in him which would restrain him from doing anything he wants.

Speaking in typological rather than in anthropological terms, the Rav regards this kind of human being as the archetype of the "one vision" man, as William Blake almost two centuries ago foresaw his emergence as a major threat to what is truly human in man. The original threat, of course, lay hidden in the Baconian dictum that in true natural philosophy there is the basis of absolutely everything. In that "everything", as Theodore Rozhak expresses himself, "there lie the dim origins of laboratory psychology and the behavioral sciences, operations research and systems analysis, general value and utility theory." In natural philosophy, according to Bacon, "human knowledge and human power meet in one." Bacon bothers to develop no other criterion of truth than the bluntly operational one. "Truth and utility," he insists, "are the very same thing." Bacon was the first, but by no means the last, of the great Europeans to call the secular future by the name of the "New philosophy"—a wholly new and domineering cultural enterprise, unintentionally foreshadowing the clearest aspects of scientized culture.

The Rav is very far from denigrating science. God, in imparting the blessing of His image on Adam the first and giving him the mandate to subdue nature, directed Adam's attention to the functional and practical aspects of his intellect through which man is able to gain control over nature. "Other intellectual inquiries, such as the metaphysical or axiologic-qualitative, no matter how incisive and penetrating, have never granted man dominion over his environment. The Greeks, who excelled in philosophical noesis, were less skillful in technological achievements. Modern science has emerged victorious from its encounter with nature because it has sacrificed qualitative-metaphysical speculation for the sake of a functional duplication of reality and substituted the *quantus* for the *qualis*" ("The Lonely Man of Faith").

Adam the first is, therefore, interested in finding an answer to the question of how the cosmos functions, and not *why* the cosmos functions at all. But even this "how" question alone was enough to confer upon man the kind of dignity which the psalmist spoke about when he said, "For Thou made him a little lower than the angels and hast crowned him with glory and dignity. . . . Thou hast made him to have dominion over the works of Thy hands . . . Thou hast put all things under his feet."

The Adam-the-first type of man, as the Rav portrays him, is "aggressive, bold, and victory minded. His motto is success, triumph over the cosmic forces." The modern scientist, as the Rav sees him, is the ideal Adam-the-first type of man, "for he does not try to explain nature; he duplicates it. In his full resplendent glory as a creative agent of God he constructs his own world, and in a mysterious fashion succeeds in controlling his environment through manipulating his own mathematical constructs and creations" ("The Lonely Man of Faith").

The Rav speaks admiringly about the greater exploits of the Adam-the-first type of man as we see and admire him today. "Driven by an urge which he cannot but obey, Adam the first transcends the limits of the reasonable and the probable and ventures into the open spaces of a boundless universe. Even this longing for vastness, no matter how adventurous and fantastic, is legitimate. Man reaching for a distant star is acting in harmony with his nature, which was created, willed, and directed by his Maker. It is a manifestation of obedience to rather than rebellion against God" ("The Lonely Man of Faith").

But there is also another side to Adam the first which expresses itself in a fascination with *exteriority*. As such he may be regarded as an aesthete, but an aesthete in the Kierkegaardian sense, that is to say, a hedonist. "Adam the first is always an aesthete, whether engaged in an intellectual or ethical performance. His conscience is energized not by the idea of the good but by that of the beautiful. His mind is questing not for the true, but for the pleasant and functional, which are rooted in the aesthetical not in the noetic-ethical sphere" ("The Lonely Man of Faith").

The Rav refers to this level of man as to one of "naturalness." The term, however, may lend itself to the wrong interpretation, for there actually is hardly anything in this man to suggest the sincerity and spontaneity of a behavior which is "natural." To the contrary, the Rav speaks here of naturalness as of an instinct-driven, success-intoxicated, expansion-oriented, socio-egocentric existence. In such a state man tends to treat real nature—nature as a source of even a temporary cathartic inspiration—impersonally, detachedly, at a distance. Heidegger speaks of this kind of man in one of his famous descriptions of "the busy busy businessman," who represents to him the embodiment of our fantastic passion for organized, exteriorized life in every area. The businessman who flies or drives to his country house for a weekend, is whisked off to golf, tennis, sailing; entertains his guests successfully, but also on a split-second schedule. At the end of the weekend he flies back to the city, but without once having had an occasion or an urge "to lose himself walking down a country lane." Such a man, we say, "is marvelously organized, and really knows how to arrange things." "And, to be sure, he does show an admirable mastery over beings, but not *being*, with which he never comes in contact. . . . To lose oneself walking down a country lane," Heidegger explains, "is literally to lose the self that is split off from nature; to enter the region of being where subject and object no longer confront each other in murderous division."

Heidegger is, of course, speaking here of an archetype of nonconfronted man, only that he seemingly sees the state of not-being-split-off-from-nature as an entrance ticket to "the region of being where subject and object no longer confront each other in murderous division." It is highly doubtful whether the Rav, for whom confronted man is at the heart of being—or, perhaps, for whom being is at the heart of the truly confronted man—would see man's intimacy with the phenomenon of nature, with what "losing oneself on a country lane" is basically all about, as a sufficient qualification for confrontedness. "The sun rises," the Rav writes, "and one sees the Almighty in the illumination of sunrise; the sun sets in an afterglow of haze, and there, too, one discerns His presence. This is a feeling that a Jew must personally experience. It does not lend itself to transmission via theological tractates and essays, homilies, and sermons. It is a feeling—and it must be experienced! I have no idea how this feeling can be instilled in American Jewry. I may not be such a bad schoolteacher, and I can give instruction on various subjects—but not on this!"

These are mighty words, for they touch upon the sensation not of "losing oneself on a country lane" but of ultimately *finding oneself* on it! How is this achieved? The psalmist, using precisely the metaphor of sunrise, provides, it seems to us, a glimpse of the right answer: "My soul yearns for the Lord more than those who watch for sunrise; yea, more than those who watch for sunrise." The phrase "those who watch for sunrise" is repeated, it seems, not just for greater emphasis, but for a vaster view of things. Rashi interprets it to mean that "I have not been discouraged by hopeful signs which prove to be unfounded; rather, I persistently watched for the morning, time and time again." What it means, in other words, is that "among those who watch for the morning," says the psalmist, "I have watched for the morning with double intensity; the intensity which is purely aesthetic and poetic and the one which transcends it by far and reaches out straight to You, my Lord!"

This state has nothing to do with man on the level of what the Rav refers to as "naturalness." What has the man who is involved with his own hedonic and pleasure-seeking nature to do with the double, or even single, sensation of sunrise? Nothing! It is of this original man that the Bible tells us that "the Lord God planted a garden eastward of Eden and there he put the man whom He had formed. And out of the ground the Lord God caused to grow every tree that is desirable to sight and good for food; the tree of life in the midst of the garden and the tree of knowledge of good and evil" (Gen. 2:8–9). A vast garden, the Rav comments, stretches before Adam the first with an almost endless variety of trees desirable and good, colorful and tempting, fascinating and exciting, the boundless fantasy of the first man.

As the Rav sees it, we are dealing here, in the biblical account of Adam the first, with the archetype of the nonconfronted man of our day and age. When he refers to man on a level of naturalness, the Rav writes, he does not have in mind the *Urmensch* of bygone times, but modern man. He is thinking, he stresses, not in anthropological, but typological categories. For nonconfronted man is to be found not only in the cave or in the jungle but in the seats of learning and in the halls of philosophers and artists. Nonconfrontation is not necessarily restricted to a primitive existence, but applies to human existence at all times, no matter how cultured and sophisticated.

ADAM THE SECOND

If Adam the first, the natural-instinctual man, moves straight ahead, along with the beasts of the field, within the limits of a "cosmic immediacy," Adam the second—be it another Adam or the same Adam who has undergone a cathartic transformation—suddenly discovers an awesome and mysterious domain which is independent of and disobedient to him. We read in Genesis 2:7: "and the eternal God formed man of the dust of the ground and breathed into his nostrils the breath of life, and man became a living soul, and the eternal God planted a garden eastwards of Eden. . . . And the eternal God took the man and placed him in the garden to serve and to keep it."

We notice that Adam the first received the mandate from God "to till the earth and subdue it." Adam the second, however, was charged with the duty "to cultivate the garden and keep it."

In the story of Adam the first, male and female are created

concurrently, while Adam the second emerges alone, with Eve appearing subsequently as a "helpmeet against him."

We also notice that in the first account of the creation of man only the Divine name *E-lohim* appears. In the second, however, *E-lohim* is used in conjunction with the Tetragrammaton. Biblical criticism has made much of this discrepancy, which, in the Rav's clear interpretation, actually comes to signify that Adam the second, who is the first human to hear a Divine command, as will be explained later, surpasses Adam the first as a *receptacle* of the Divine norm.

We also notice, as the Rav teaches us, another vital difference between the two Adams. In the case of Adam the first, we read that he was placed (*vayassem*) in the garden of Eden for one purpose only—to pursue pleasure. We deal here, as mentioned, with a non-normative being who was not yet on the receiving side of the Divine command ("And God commanded" is an Adam-the-second attribute). When it comes to Adam the second, however, the term used, *vayikah* ("and He took") suggests *dislocation*. He was, that is, dislocated from his position of naturalness and harmonious being and placed in a new existential realm. "Confronted man," the Rav boldly states, "is a displaced person. . . . Having been taken out (*vayikah*) from a state of complacency and optimistic naivete he finds the ultimate relationship between him and the order of facticity ending in tension and conflict. . . . At this stage man, estranged from nature, fully aware of his grand and tragic destiny, becomes the recipient of the first norm: 'And the Lord commanded man . . .' " ("Confrontation").

Man, removed into another dimension where he is subjected to the call of the norm, can no longer be passive. He is seized by a dialectical tension which is the source of his energy, his anxiety, and above all, his creativity. It is an elevated but precarious position. It is also one of enormous responsibility. The Bible speaks of the responsibility placed on man once he marches no longer with the beasts of the field: man is suddenly confronted not only with a conscious self, but with a conscious need to bring order into everything outside of himself. "And out of the ground the Lord God formed every beast of the field and every fowl of the air, and brought them unto Adam to see what he would call them, and whatever Adam called every living creature, that was the name thereof'' (Gen. 2:19).

Here, one might say, begins human creativity. Only of God are we told in the Psalms that He gave names to all celestial bodies. What this elevation of man to the rank of co-creator means, as has been observed by Prof. Harvey Cox of Harvard Divinity School, is that "creation is not completed by God in the Bible until after man is formed and begins to work as partner of the Creator in bringing order to the chaos and giving form to the formless. . . . God, in other words, does not simply insert man into a world filled with creatures that are already named in relationships and meaning-patterns already established by decrees" (*The Secular City*).[1]

AND GOD COMMANDED

Man as a normative creature begins with Adam the second. It is he who hears for the first time a Divine command. "And the Lord commanded . . ." (Gen. 2:16). "What does this categorical command mean?" the Rav asks. It means, he replies, that with the birth of the norm, man is suddenly "aware of his singularly human existence which expresses itself in the dichotomous experience of being unfree, restricted, imperfect, and unredeemed and, at the same time, being potentially powerful, great and exalted, uniquely endowed and capable to rise far above his environment in response to the Divine challenge" ("The Lonely Man of Faith").

Simultaneously with man's realization of his inner incongruity and alienation from his environment, the human tragic destiny begins to unfold. It begins to unfold, as said, not with original sin, but, as the Rav stresses, with an original Divine command which renders man uneasy, even unhappy with his supervised station in the world. In his perplexity and fear he is suddenly faced with loneliness. And it is at this stage where the third level to which man, longing for self-fulfillment, must ascend, comes into prominence. It is a confrontation of a different kind, however. It is not,

---

1. Prof. Cox rightly states that "generations of scholars, charmed by the spell of Greek philosophy, have simply overlooked this astonishing fact." Overlooked, by the way, by most Christian theologians!

in the Rav's words, "the confrontation of a subject who gazes with a sense of superiority at an object beneath him, but of two equal subjects both lonely in their otherness and uniqueness, both opposed and rejected by an objective order, both craving for companionship. The confrontation is reciprocal, not unilateral. This time the two confronters stand alongside each other. An aloof existence is transformed into a together existence" ("Confrontation").

The Rav quotes in this context from Genesis 2:18–22: " 'It is not good that the man should be alone. I will make a helpmate opposite him. . . . And the Lord God made the rib which He had taken from the man into a woman, and He brought her unto man.' God created Eve, another human being. Two individuals, lonely and helpless in their solitude, meet, and the first community is formed" ("Confrontation").

In "The Lonely Man of Faith" the Rav introduces us to two communities of man whom we can genealogically and ontologically trace to the two Adams: the first, traceable to the first Adam, is, as the Rav calls it, "the natural work community," and the second, "the covenantal faith community." The Divine maxim that "it is not good for man to be alone" may apply to both communities, but it seems that they do not interpret it, or, more exactly do not experience it in the same manner.

IT IS NOT GOOD FOR MAN TO BE ALONE

"The covenantal faith community," the Rav writes, "in contradistinction to the natural work community, interprets the Divine pronouncement 'It is not good for man to be alone,' not in utilitarian, but in ontological terms; *it is not good for man to be lonely* (not alone), with emphasis placed upon 'to be.' Being at the level of the faith community does not lend itself to any equation. 'To be' is not to be equated with 'to work and produce goods' (as historical materialism wants us to believe). 'To be' is not identical with 'to think' (as the classical tradition of philosophical rationalism throughout the ages, culminating in Descartes and later in Kant, try to convince us). 'To be' does not exhaust itself either in suffering (as Schopenhauer preached) or in enjoying the world of sense (in accordance with ethical hedonism). 'To be' is a unique in-depth experience of which only Adam the second is aware, and is unrelated to any function or performance. 'To be' means to be the only one, singular and different and, consequently, lonely. For what causes man to be lonely and feel insecure if not the awareness of his uniqueness and exclusiveness? The 'I' is lonely, experiencing ontological incompleteness and causalness because there is no one who exists like the 'I', and because the *modus existentiae* of the 'I' cannot be repeated, imitated or experienced by others" ("The Lonely Man of Faith").

It is, therefore, no accident that loneliness appears on the human scene together with Adam the second. Adam the second must quest, in the Rav's words, for a different kind of community from the natural work community, as prefigured by Adam the first. "His quest is for a new kind of fellowship which one finds in the existential community. . . . There not only hands are joined but experiences as well; there one hears not only the rhythmic sound of the production line, but also the rhythmic beat of hearts starved for existential companionship and all-embracing sympathy, and experiencing the grandeur of the faith community; there one lonely soul finds another soul tormented by loneliness and solitude, yet unqualifiedly committed" ("The Lonely Man of Faith").

This leads the Rav to the conclusion that the sense of loneliness is an existential attribute, and that its overcoming can take place only in an encounter between one "numinous, in-depth personality" and another.

I doubt whether anybody has managed to better define the true meaning of a *redemptive* dialogue. Dialogue for the Rav means a numinous experience which is unthinkable without the partners to the dialogue being armed with the cognitive power of a light from within. This leads the Rav to the conclusion—a conclusion whose veracity can be attested to by the life stories of the numinous, in-depth personalities of halakhic men down the ages—that friendship, true dialogical friendship, is possible only when the thirst for a dialogue is quenched by communication as an experience of a creative, cognitive exchange. "Friendship," the Rav writes in truth, "—not as a social surface relation, but as an existential in-depth relation between two individuals—is realizable only within the framework of the covenantal community where in-depth personalities relate themselves to each other ontologically and where total commitment to God and fellow men is the order of the day. In the majestic community (of Adam the first) in which surface personalities meet, and commitment never exceeds the bounds of the utilitarian, we may find collegiality, neighborliness, civility, or courtesy, but not friendship, which is the exclusive experience awarded by God to the covenantal man who is thus redeemed from his agonizing solitude'' ("The Lonely Man of Faith").

Solitude appears here, as mentioned earlier, as an Adam-the-second typicality. It is what singles him out as a creature on a higher level of consciousness. The Adam-the-first type of man, however, seems to treat the problem of loneliness, inasmuch as it bothers him, as he treats boredom: by exposing himself to one manifestation or another of "action culture," that is to say, to something that would act *on* him from without—something visual, funny, noisy, etc. Solitude, existential solitude, is definitely not a common experience. The very experience of solitude bears testimony to a higher state of consciousness. It is, therefore, surprising that Paul Tillich, the Christian philosopher-theologian, regarded existential loneliness—and I stress existential—as a malaise that afflicts *everybody*. "Who has not at some time," he writes, "been lonely in the midst of a social event? The feeling of our separation from the rest of life is most acute when we are surrounded by it in noise and talk. We realize then much more than in moments of solitude how strange we are to each other, how estranged life is from life. Each one of us draws back into himself. He cannot penetrate the hidden center of another individual; nor can that individual pass beyond the shroud that covers our own being. Even the greatest love cannot break through the walls of the self" (*The Shaking of the Foundations*).

The Rav does not see the Adam-the-first type of man as bothered at all by such existential problems. Adam-the-first type of man experiences loneliness as a void in time, not in himself or in life. His problem is therefore best expressed in three terrible words: "to kill time." On the extreme opposite side of killing time there arises the great need of *confronting* it. "Not even the greatest love can break through the walls of the self." There are moments, however, moments of true and tragic confrontation, when man can, to use an expression of Kafka's, "feel his own depth."

The Rav speaks of loneliness—not aloneness, but loneliness—

the way Tillich, somehow contradicting his previous statement about existential loneliness as a common experience, speaks of anxiety, quite often the companion of solitude. "God speaks to man through anxiety, which is expressive of estrangement." To Heidegger, too, anxiety results from man's realization of himself being "thrown into the world" and of "the unalterable finitude of his life." Both these descriptions of anxiety apply to a large degree to existential solitude as seen by the Rav. "I despair," the Rav writes, "because I am lonely and hence feel frustrated. On the other hand, I also feel invigorated because this very experience of loneliness presses everything in me into the service of God. In my 'desolate, howling solitude' I am experiencing a growing awareness that, to paraphrase Plotinus' apothegm about prayer, this service to which I, a lonely and solitary individual, am committed is wanted and gracefully accepted by God in His transcendental loneliness and numinous solitude."

A HELPMEET AGAINST HIM

The third level which man, longing for self-fulfillment, must ascend is, as the Rav sees it, a confrontation of a different kind; this time, however, it is not, as aforementioned, "the confrontation of a subject who gazes with a sense of superiority at the object beneath him, but of two equal subjects, both lonely in their otherness and uniqueness, and both craving for companionship. The confrontation is thus reciprocal, not unilateral. This time the two confronters stand alongside each other. An aloof existence is transformed into a together existence." How does this come to pass? By the power of the word. "Out of the mystery of original muteness, the miraculous word is first heard, the first act of communication. Adam suddenly begins to speak: 'And the man said.' We don't know what he said, but we do know that out of the opening words, whatever they were, two fenced in, isolated human existences ecstatically broke through to each other" ("The Lonely Man of Faith").

The word, says the Rav, is a paradoxical instrument of communication. It contains an inner contradiction. On the one hand, the word is the medium of expressing agreement and understanding. On the other hand, however, the word is also the means of manifesting distinctness and differences of opinion. The word brings out not only what is common to two existences, but the uniqueness and singularity of each existence. The word is the carrier of enormous power. It can enlighten, and it can confound; it can revive and it can kill. We must therefore assume that the Creator, who endowed the first couple with the power of the word, also endowed them with the ability for a dialectical relationship, as expressed in the word, and in the spirit of "a helpmeet against him." Writes the Rav: "The hope of finding a personal, existential equation of two human beings is rooted in the dangerous and false notion that human existences are abstract magnitudes, subject to simple mathematical processes. The error lies at the root of the philosophies of the corporate and of mechanistic behaviorism. In fact, the closer two individuals get to know each other, the more aware are they of the metaphysical distance that separates them. . . . The sun of existence rises with the birth of one's self-awareness and sets with its termination" ("The Lonely Man of Faith").[2]

A STRANGER AND A SOJOURNER IN YOUR MIDST

Patriarch Abraham reaches the peak of confrontation—for himself and for all generations of his descendants—when he speaks these few simple words to the idolators around him: "I am a stranger and a sojourner in your midst." This second great dialectical statement in Scripture—the first being, "a helpmeet against him"—induces the Rav to pose the question whether it is possible to be "a stranger and a sojourner" at the same time? "Is not this definition absurd, since it contravenes the central principle of classical logic that no cognitive judgment may contain two mutually exclusive terms?" The Rav's answer is existentialist to the core:

2. The reason usually given for divorce is "irreconcilable differences." But how does one know how to determine the "irreconcilability" of differences if there are differences that one can only learn to distinguish, and that are, in fact, vital for a dialectical, "helpmeet against him" togetherness? How do they know that what they call "irreconcilable differences" are not, in the ontological sense, irreconcilable nondifferences—sameness, predictability, boredom, vacuity?

" 'A helpmeet against him' and 'a stranger and sojourner in your midst' both point toward the tragic but heroic dichotomy in human nature and history," the latter as manifested with particular force in the covenantal faith community—the Jewish people.

In other words, "The greatness of man manifests itself in his dialectical approach to his confronter, in ambivalent acting toward his fellow man, in giving friendship and hurling defiance, in relating himself to and, at the same time, retreating from him. In the dichotomy of a 'helpmeet against him' we find our triumph as well as our defeat" ("Confrontation").

And we find ourselves as confronted human beings!

ADAM THE SECOND AS PROTOTYPE OF THE STRANGER AND SOJOURNER IN YOUR MIDST

Exactly as man in the life of the mass order, that is to say, in the leveled-down culture of the generality which tends to conform to the demands of the average human being, would never know the dialectical meaning of a "helpmeet against him," so would the alienated Jew, as indeed, the unlearned non-Jew, never understand the meaning of "A stranger and a sojourner I am in your midst." Only confronted man and confronted Jew—and the Jew's is actually a double confrontation!—can grasp, as an example, the reason why the Rav does not hesitate to state on various occasions that the homo religiosus can be, and quite often is, alas, a nonconfronted man! He comes to a place of worship, attends lectures on religion, listens attentively to the rabbi's sermons, and enjoys the ceremonial, yet, says the Rav, he is searching not for a faith in all its singularity and otherness, but for religious "culture." He seeks not the greatness found in sacrificial action, but the convenience one discovers in a serene, comfortable state of mind. He sees an aesthetic experience rather than a convenantal one, a social ethos rather than a Divine imperative.

The Rav describes as "diabolical" the insistence of Western man upon being successful. "Alas, he wants to be successful even in his adventure with God! If he gives of himself to God he expects reciprocity. He also reaches a covenant with God, but this covenant is a mercantile one. In a primitive manner, he wants to trade 'favors' and exchange 'goods.' The gesture of faith to him is a give-and-take affair, and reflects the philosophy of Job which led to catastrophe—a philosophy which sees faith as a quid pro quo arrangement and expects compensation for each sacrifice one offers. That is why modern man puts up demands that faith adapt itself to the mood and temper of modern times" ("The Lonely Man of Faith").

But what is faith? A confession? A ceremony? A convenience? A sacrament? A ritual? A sentiment? Judaism refuses to provide a formula for faith, but it points at the road—very long and tortuous—that leads there. It took a Nazi concentration camp to convince Dietrich Bonhoeffer, the German martyr-priest hanged by the Nazis, that there was something intolerable about the Christian notion of "easy grace." Judaism juxtaposes it with the eternal symbolism of Jacob's wrestling with God. "The untranslatability of the complete faith experience," the Rav says, "is due not to the weakness but to the strength of the latter" ("The Lonely Man of Faith").

But if the complete faith experience does not lend itself to an easy "translatability," to any fixation, its opposite, namely the immediacy-experience of the natural work community, is clearly identifiable. And it is probably in this area that existentialism has established itself as the most persuasive observer of the human scene. Those who express the opinion that existentialism has lost some of its vigor are simply overlooking the fact that existentialism, as a philosophy of crisis, has proven itself more equipped than any other trend of thought to define the symptoms of the present-day human predicament. All existential philosophers, from Kierkegaard to the Rav, not only show the same aversion for mediocrity, but point in the same direction of its flagrantly manifested symptoms. Karl Jaspers spells it out: "The life of the mass order, going hand in hand with the culture of the generality," tends to conform to the demands of the average human being, that is to say, of mediocrity. That is how "spirituality" is being diffused among the masses when knowledge is impoverished in every possible way by rationalization until it becomes accessible to the crude understanding of all. As a result of this leveling-down process—a characteristic of the life order—there is a tendency toward the disappearance of that stratum of cultural persons who have come into being thanks to a continuous disciplining of their thoughts and feelings which renders them capable of mental creation. "It seems," Jaspers writes, "as if the world must be given over to mediocrities, to persons without a destiny, without a rank, or difference, without genuinely human attributes. . . . Oblivion is the basis of such a life whose outlooks upon past and present shrink so much that scarcely anything remains but the bald present" (*Man in the Modern Age*).

What shrinks in this process is also the chance to hope for a change. It is truly astonishing how difficult it has become to confront hope—yes, hope!—as a real possibility for a better world and a better man even when everything seems to point in promising directions. But, as Jacques Ellul, the inspired Frenchman, put it, "there is no hope where suspicion is king. Every time a possibility, a breakthrough, or a meaning takes shape, immediately the question bursts in upon us, 'from what social class, from what complex, from what ideology, from what myth, from what interest does this hope spring, since it is nothing but the falsification of a situation one has refused to face' " (*Hope in Time of Abandonment*).

That is to say, refused to confront.

That is why it is only when ontological falsification is extradited that confrontation can come into prominence. But a great deal of knowledge is needed in order to know how to *defalsify* situations! The same is true of friendship: something radical must happen to the inner life of true friends for one to crave the truth—not just the presence but the truth—of the other! It is not in vain that the Rav maintains that friendship—not as social surface relations, but "as an existential, in-depth communication between two individuals— is realizable only within the framework of the covenantal faith community wherein depth personalities relate themselves to each other ontologically, and total commitment to God and his fellow men is the order of the day" ("The Lonely Man of Faith").

And here the Rav makes a statement which requires commentary. "Modern man," the Rav states, "who did not meet to the fullest the challenge of confrontation on the second level, does not perform well on the level of personal confrontation either." I wonder whether this powerful psychological insight into the present-day human condition has been adequately appreciated even by ardent disciples of the Rav. For what the Rav implies here is that without the yardstick necessary for self-evaluation provided by the Adam-the-second state of mind, we may be simply incapable of grasping the nature of even our most mundane problems.

We shall better understand the acuteness of this insight if we resort to a quotation from a remarkable psychiatrist, the late Abraham Maslow: "When the shallow life doesn't work, and is questioned, then there is a call for fundamentals." Thousands of marriages are going on the rocks only because the shallow life does not work, and is not questioned. For how can one be expected to question the shallow life without doing away with shallowness, and how can one do away with shallowness without some form of what the Rav calls catharsis, or confrontation? But catharsis and confrontation are already phenomena of a different order: the order of Adam the second.

Thus the Rav's observation that modern man, who did not meet the challenge of confrontation on the second level, does not perform well on the level of personal confrontation either, is exact. One must be what William James calls "a wider self" in order to be able to adequately cope with the smaller self in him. What it amounts to is that exactly as Adam the first will not perform well on his level without having met in some way the challenge of confrontation on the second level, Adam the second will not perform well on his level without having met some typical challenges of Adam the first. It thus follows that when man gives himself to the covenantal faith community, the Halakhah, a life-affirming proposition, reminds him, as the Rav puts it, "that he is wanted and needed in another community, the natural one." And when he comes across man who is involved in the creative enterprise of Adam the first—and Adam the first can be very creative!—he does not let him forget that he is "a covenantal being who will never find self-fulfillment outside of the covenant."

If the fulfillment of faith is born, in the Rav's words, out of "the intrusion of eternity upon temporality," and its prime goal is "redemption from the inadequacies of the finite and mainly from the flux of temporality," then we are dealing here with a confrontation which must never be regarded in any way as a renunciation. "Redemption from the inadequacies of the finite," as the Rav puts it, is by no means redemption from, or renunciation of, the finite as a whole, only from its inadequacies. The self-tortured saints and recluses of Christianity may belong to an Adam-the-second category, but having rejected completely the Adam-the-first involvement with the finite, it was inevitable that many of them would consign themselves to a confrontation of a very special kind: the violent confrontation with their flesh!

THE DOUBLE CONFRONTATION

Confronted man, i.e., the man of double confrontation—a typicality of the covenantal faith community—is also the carrier of a double load of concern for himself and for the world. The so-called Jewish ferment, the restlessness of the Jews, and, to quote Isaac Bashevis Singer, "their inability to sleep well and their not letting the rest of the world sleep well either," may very well be the result of their "genetic" double confrontation. If the doubly confronted Jew were to raise the question of Matriarch Rebecca: "What do I need it for?"—meaning the double load in her womb—the answer would be similar to that which was given to her by God Himself: she was carrying within herself not just two persons, but two worlds—different, at odds, one sometimes stronger, sometimes weaker than the other—but in the long run the seemingly weaker, but spiritually stronger, will prevail.

But the most difficult confrontation of them all is not between Jacob and Esau, but between Jacob and Jacob, i.e., between Jacob and himself. The Rav speaks about it with an astonishing frankness: "In the long life journey, at one point or another, one must reach the absurd stage at which one finds oneself bankrupt and forlorn. The Bible, with ruthless honesty, recorded such experiences of failure in the lives of our greatest. Man must be cognizant of this tragic fact, which sooner or later he must encounter if his metaphysical destiny is to be realized. Great is not the man who has never faltered but the man who tripped, fell, and rose again to greater heights. Sin is a reality, not just a potential threat. Perfect man has never been created. If man is not conscious of the contradiction inherent in the very core of his personality, he lives in the world of illusions and leads an unredeemed existence" ("Catharsis").

That is to say, a non-confronted life!

Jacob, who, more than the other two Patriarchs, prefigures the history of Israel, is the confronted man par excellence. His was indeed a double confrontation, as were the Jews of old. The so-called emancipated modern Jew has been trying for a long time, in the Rav's words, "to do away with his twofold responsibility, which weighs heavily upon him," for he maintains that "it is impossible to engage in both confrontations, the universal and the covenantal, which, in his opinion, are mutually exclusive. It is, he argues, absurd to stand shoulder to shoulder with mankind preoccupied with the cognitive-technological gesture for the welfare of all, implementing the mandate granted to us by the Creator, and to make an about face the next minute in order to confront our comrades as a distinct and separate community. Hence, the Western Jew concludes, we have to choose between two encounters. We are either confronted human beings or confronted Jews. A double confrontation contains an inner contradiction" ("Confrontation").

And it does! That was precisely the inner contradiction that is contained in the few monumental words with which Patriarch Abraham forever established the sacred differentness of the Jew as a doubly confronted being: "A stranger and a sojourner am I in your midst."

These few words contain the secret of Jewish uniqueness. "And there can be no identity without uniqueness" ("Confrontation").

3

The Royal Road and the Narrow Ridge

If man's sense of nothingness, unworthiness, and nonbeing is manifested by—or hidden in—the feeling of sin, sin is indeed a sickness. Kierkegaard spoke of this seemingly strange, irrational "symbiosis" of sin and sickness in the very middle of a century— the nineteenth—which enthusiastically embraced rationalism and, along with it, the biological interpretation of man. By now we realize that that interpretation, as is the case with psychoanalysis, narrowed the case for man's personal unhappiness down to the person himself in his formative years. Nobody denies that there is some validity to this claim, but, as the existentialists put it, psychology found out something important about neurotic guilt, or circumstantial, exaggerated, unscrutinized personal guilt, but it did not have anything to say about real or natural creature-guilt. It tried to lay a total claim on the problem of unhappiness when it actually had only a partial claim on the problem. Otto Rank, who may very well have surpassed his master and erstwhile colleague, Sigmund Freud, therefore stated very clearly that "psychology, which is gradually trying to supplant religious and moral ideology, is only partially qualified to do this because it is predominantly a negative and disintegrating ideology."

Why so? Because since psychology narrows the case for personal unhappiness down to the person himself, he is then stuck with himself—often to the point of suffocation. The highly versatile Ernest Becker (in his *Denial of Death*) puts it this way: "All the analysis in the world doesn't allow a person to find out who he is and why he is here on earth; why he had to die and how he can make his life a triumph. It is when psychology tries to do this, when it offers itself as a full explanation of human unhappiness that it becomes a fraud and makes the situation of modern man an impasse from which he cannot escape.''

This impasse, in other words, was created by modern man himself. It started with the great sweep of scientific optimism about man that typified the nineteenth century, a century in which man hoped to find ''immortality'' in a new and secure way. He desired a heroic apotheosis, as did all other historical men, but now, after a series of setbacks of man's confidence in his ability to work out his own salvation, there is no one to give that apotheosis to him except his psychological guru. In this sense, Rank asserts with uncanny insight, psychologists ''are, so to say, the neurotic's product of his illness.'' Modern man needs a ''thou'' to whom to turn for spiritual and moral guidance, and, as God was ''in eclipse,'' the therapist had to replace him. Ernest Becker writes: ''For a long time now, the psychoanalysts, not understanding this historical problem, have been trying to figure out why the termination of the 'transference' in therapy is such a devilish problem in many cases. Had they read and understood Rank they would quickly have seen that the 'thou' of the therapist is the new God who must replace the old collective ideologies of redemption. As the individual cannot serve as God, he must give rise to a truly devilish problem. Modern man is condemned to seek the meaning of his life in psychological introspection, and so his new confessor has to be the supreme authority on introspection. As this is so, the patient's 'beyond' is limited to the analytic couch and the world view imparted there.''

In this sense, as Otto Rank saw it first hand, psychoanalysis actually stultifies the emotional life of the patient. ''Man,'' in Becker's words, ''wants to focus his love on the absolute measure of power and value, and the analyst tells him that all is reducible to his early conditioning and is therefore relative. Man wants to find and experience the marvelous, and the analyst tells him how matter of fact everything is, how clinically explainable are our deepest ontological motives and guilts. Man is thereby deprived of the absolute mystery he needs, and the only omnipotent thing that then remains is the man who explained it away. And so the patient clings to his analyst with all his might and dreads terminating the analysis.''

RANK, KIERKEGAARD, AND THE RAV

Becker was right when he said that the further one pushes his study of Rank, the more his writings blur into those of Kierkegaard. This blurring of Rank and Kierkegaard, however, is not a meek surrender to ideology, but an actual scientific working-through of the problems of human character. Following the most exhaustive psychological search, both men reached the conclusion that at the very furthest reaches of scientific description psychology has to give way to theology, that is to say, to a world-view which absorbs the individual's conflicts and guilts and offers him some kind of ''heroic apotheosis.''

That heroic apotheosis is *exactly* what the Rav means by, and how he actually describes, *teshuvah* (repentance). This will be the subject of our inquiry as we proceed. For the moment, let us try to introduce the Rav's unique concept of *teshuvah* by means of the ''good offices,'' as it were, of Rank and Kierkegaard. It was Ernest Becker of Yale who first discovered the amazing affinity of thought between two great psychologists who lived a century-and-a-half apart. ''Here,'' Becker writes, ''Rank and Kierkegaard meet in one of those astonishing historical mergers of thought—that sin and neurosis are two ways of talking about the same thing: the complete isolation of the individual; his disharmony with the rest of nature, his hyperindividualism, his attempts to create his own world from within himself. Neurosis, like sin, is an attempt to force nature, to pretend that the *causa-sui* project really suffices. In sin as in neurosis man fetishizes himself on something narrow at hand and pretends that the whole meaning and miraculousness of creation is limited to that; that he can get his satisfaction from it.''

Otto Rank spells this out with even greater clarity: ''The neurotic type suffers from a consciousness of sin just as much as did his religious ancestor, without, however, believing in the *conception* of sin. This is precisely what makes him 'neurotic': he feels as a sinner without the religious belief in sin, for which he therefore needs a new rational explanation" (quoted in Ernest Becker's *Denial of Death*).

HEROIC APOTHEOSIS

"Heroic apotheosis" is one way of defining the kind of therapy which the sin-sickness or sin-neurosis seeks; "catharsis" is another. The Rav uses both, but the latter is the name of one of his remarkable essays on the subject. The Rav, to better explain catharsis, speaks of the difference between two seemingly interchangeable Hebrew words so often mentioned in the Bible and in the prayers: *ko'aḥ* and *gevurah*. *Ko'aḥ* is physical strength. It denotes any aptitude which God has bestowed upon man at birth; it is the capability to perform work which requires an unusual amount of physical vigor. As such, it is not an exclusively human category. Since the beast shares with man all his organic aptitudes, the category of *ko'aḥ* is applicable to man and beast alike.

Gevurah is different. *Gevurah*, or heroism, in contradistinction to *ko'aḥ*, is, in the Rav's words, "an exclusive grant of God to man which demonstrates the latter's unique position in creation—man's charismatic endowment, and his chosenness. *Gevurah*, in the context of the biblical narrative and hymns, denotes the capacity of attaining victory, of defeating a foe who engages one in combat. However, the victory with which *gevurah* is identified is not military victory alone. On the contrary, at times, the warrior who is defeated on the battlefield emerges as the *gibor*, the hero, as, for example, is the case with Samson."

Gevurah, as the Rav sees it, is something which is inversely related to *ko'aḥ*, to the degree of the might one has at his disposal. The greater the force one wields, the less *gevurah* one needs to display. Conversely, the weaker one is, the tougher the odds, the more exalted is the action of the hero, the *gibor*. For the real hero, as the Rav sees it, disregards practical reasoning and resorts to the "absurd."

Only on a few occasions does the Rav introduce the existential notion of the absurd into his terminology, and when he does mention it, it appears more as an "as if" than as an actual description of a given situation, as is the case, for example, in

Sartre's famous "absurd existence." The interesting point about the Rav's use of the absurd is the fact that he uses it to better define *gevurah*. A new element is introduced into the gesture of *gevurah*, namely, heroism as "action undertaken contrary to human logic and human practical judgment." This kind of action, however, if undertaken for a great, just cause, quite often leads to ultimate victory. "There are situations in life with which clear-cut logical processes and utilitarian approaches fail to cope, while the sudden, spontaneous leap into the absurd may save man when he finds himself in utter distress and despair. This nonpractical nonrational action is heroic, though absurd," and is identified with *gevurah*.

The highest, most heroic, and indeed most noble example of *gevurah* is contained in the story which may very well prefigure the entire history as well as metahistory of the Jewish people: Jacob's "wrestling with God." We should add here that the name which Jacob was given by the celestial being he wrestled with, "Israel," is prophecy at its most powerful and identifiable—from eternity to here. The name alone contains the essence of a history written in advance, as Nachmanides defined the Bible as a whole.

Jacob, the Rav writes (in "Catharsis"), has emerged victorious from a most awesome encounter. He had held fast to his mysterious foe through the night of sorrow, fear, and loneliness until the new day dawned, and though wounded, he emerged victorious. "Was Jacob's victory something to be expected? Could it have been predicted logically? Was he certain of victory? Of course, not! He was alone, weak and unarmed, a novice in the art of warfare. Why did Jacob not surrender to the foe who attacked him in the night?"

And the Rav replies: "Jacob acted 'absurdly' and contrary to all rational practical considerations. In other words, he acted heroically. He, the lonely and helpless Jacob, dared engage a mighty adversary in combat. He who displayed so much business acumen and the keenness of a pragmatic mind during his long sojourn in Laban's household, suddenly, in the darkness of a grisly, strange night, made the leap into the 'absurd.' He refused to yield to superior force and declared war upon an invincible enemy. What Jacob displayed," the Rav concludes, "was not *ko'aḥ* but *gevurah*—heroism which is always employed when reason despairs and logic retreats. With daybreak, the helpless, lonely nonlogical Jacob found himself unexpectedly the victor, the hero.''

In other words, "absurd" heroism—not logic—won the day!

GREEK TRAGEDY AND WRESTLING WITH GOD

The Rav remarks at this juncture that the narrative about Jacob's heroism is totally different from the classical type of heroism which has come down to us from Greek tragedy. For classical man, heroism was intrinsically an aesthetic category which fascinated with its grandeur and glory. True, the aesthetic hero suffered from a sense of frustration at his inability to cross the Rubicon separating finitude from infinity. That is why, in his agony, he invented the image of the hero. The mere myth of the hero gave him endless comfort. The hero of classical man, as was the case with Greek tragedy, was the grandiose figure with whom, in order to satisfy his endless vanity, classical man identified himself. The aesthetic hero is therefore intrinsically dramatic and theatrical. The classical heroic gesture represented frightened disenchanted man who tries to achieve immortality by identifying himself with the heroic figure on the stage. It does not represent a way of life. It lasts for a while, vibrant and forceful, but soon man reverts to the nonheroic mood of daily life.

By everlasting contrast, biblical heroism, as prefigured by Jacob wrestling with a celestial being in the night, is not nurtured by an ephemeral mood and passing state of mind. Generations of Jews lived by its symbol and promise for woe and weal alike, by the wound as by the victory which finally came when "dawn breaketh." "It is perhaps," the Rav writes, "the central motive of our existential experience. It pervades the human man steadily and imparts to him a strange feeling of tranquility. The heroic person, according to our view, does not succumb to frenzy and excitement. Biblical heroics is not ecstatic, but rather contemplative. . . . The individual, instead of undertaking heroic action sporadically, lives constantly as a hero. Jacob did not just act heroically upon the spur of the moment; his action was indicative of a *resolute* way of life. He was not out to impress anybody. This type of heroics lasts as long as man is aware of himself as a singular being.''

The question arises here, Why did Jacob grant his attacker the freedom he pleaded for? "Release me, I pray, for the morning star hath risen.'' The vanquished adversary, as the Rav points out, did not even promise Jacob that he would not repeat his attack, nor did he apologize for what he had done. "To release such a dangerous fiend was 'unreasonable.' [But] this very unreasonableness endowed the act with the quality of the heroic, *and may serve as a pattern for halakhic heroism.*''

We shall deal more broadly with the Rav's seemingly enigmatic view of what he refers to as "halakhic heroism'' in another chapter. At this stage we are concerned with *teshuvah* as a halakhic prescription for and definition of *gevurah*.

HALAKHIC HEROISM AS THE ABILITY TO RETREAT

Jacob did not pursue his victory to the end. He retreated. The Rav sees in this retreat from a victory well in sight a condition for spiritual advance. The idea of retreating from a victory which is close at hand is, as the Rav sees it, the essence of catharsis, the dialectical movement which manifests itself in all halakhic norms regulating human life.

How does the Rav explain it? "Nowhere does the doctrine of dialectical catharsis assert itself more frequently than it does in the aesthetic hedonic realm.''

Man, the Rav says, purges himself in this realm by engaging in a dialectical movement, that is to say, by withdrawing at the moment when passion reaches its peak. "The more intoxicating and bewildering the prospect of hedonic gratification, the greater the redemptive capacity of the dialectical catharsis—of the movement of recoil.''

The Rav's halakhic example of this creative act of dialectical catharsis is remarkable for its manifold implications, halakhic and emotional. He speaks in maximum terms, but even minimally they hold a vital truth: Bride and bridegroom are young, physically strong, and passionately in love. The wedding festivities are over and they are finally alone, yearning for each other's embrace.

Suddenly there is a movement of recoil. He must not touch her. Why? She is ritually "unclean." The man, "like a chivalrous knight," exhibits "paradoxical heroism," as the Rav puts it. "He takes his own defeat. There is no glamour attached to the withdrawal. Nor is there a witness to admire and laud it. It happened in the sheltered privacy of the couple's home, in the stillness of the night. Like Jacob of old, the young man makes an about-face; he retreats when fulfillment seems assured."

The Rav goes on to explain that this kind of dialectical discipline is not limited to man's sexual life, but extends to all areas of natural drive and temptation. The hungry person must forgo the pleasure of taking certain foods, no matter how strong the temptation; men of property must forgo the pleasure of acquisition if it is morally and halakhically wrong. "In short, the Halakhah requires of man that he possess the capability for withdrawal" ("Catharsis").

The Rav goes even further with his theory of withdrawal, or "retreat," as a halakhic and, indeed, existential postulate, stating that "the cathartic act consists in retreating or disengaging from oneself, from one's inner world, in renouncing something that is part of oneself such as a sentiment, a mood, or a state of mind." The Rav asserts that Halakhah answers in the affirmative to the question of whether man is capable of dismissing even an overpowering experience. Laws such as "thou shall not covet" or "thou shall not hate thy brother," etc., are an integral part of the halakhic normative system, as are those related to human external action. Of course, one cannot possibly reach such a state of perfection and selfhood without being a halakhic man, for there is a direct connection between the knowledge of the Torah and character perfection. It is not only, as the Rav says, that according to Halakhah, catharsis in the emotional sphere consists in active human interference with the emotive experience; it also consists of the halakhah experience making this active human interference with the emotive process possible.

The Rav, totally committed to the idea of inner withdrawal or emotional catharsis as paradigmatic to the Halakhah, resorts, as an example, to the otherwise puzzling biblical account of Aaron's loss of his two sons, Nadav and Avihu. Tragedy struck on the most joyous day of Aaron's life, when the Tabernacle was dedicated and he was inaugurated into the office of high priest. Following the death of Aaron's two sons, Moses enjoined his brother and his surviving sons from mourning over the loss. In the original Hebrew text there are *two* words that Moses said to his brother by way of explanation and consolation: *bikrovai ekadesh*. In translation (King James Version), they mean: "This *is it* that the Lord spoke, saying: I will be sanctified in them that come nigh to Me." Aaron's reaction, too, is expressed in two words: *vayidom Aharon*—"And Aaron fell silent" (Lev. 10:3).

We have no way to understand how Moses' two words to his shattered brother, who has just lost his two illustrious sons, could have been enough to make him keep his peace, unless we realize two things. First, Moses' two words summarized or hinted at a relationship between the God of Israel and those who are "nigh Him" which is extraordinarily demanding."[1] Second, and this is what the Rav was after in resorting to this great and puzzling event, Moses' two seemingly mysterious words were enough for Aaron, the High Priest, to immediately undergo a movement of "recoil." *Vayidom Aharon*—"And Aaron held his peace."

The Rav elaborates on this subject: The priests constituted a community of the anointed who were consecrated exclusively to the service of God, as it is written, "for the anointing oil of the Lord is upon them." But is this why the inalienable right to which every parent is entitled—the right to mourn the death of a child— was denied to Aaron and his other children? So it seems, anyway: "The commitment of consecration of a priest to God is all-demand- ing, all-inclusive. God lays unrestricted claim not to part but to the whole of the human personality." What does this mean in emo- tional and psychological terms? It means, says the Rav, "that God wanted Aaron to disown the strongest emotion in man—the love of a child! Is it possible? As far as modern man is concerned, I would not dare answer. With respect to biblical man, we read that Aaron acted in accord with the Divine instruction."

The dialectical catharsis is here manifested to the maximum in

---

1. It should not be regarded as a homiletical commentary if we state at this juncture that the entire idea of chosenness assumes, in view of this tragic event, a terrifying significance. The Lord God is infinitely stricter with those who are "nigh" Him than with others! And this is not only a matter of priests. Does it not say that "you shall be unto Me a kingdom of priests, a holy people?"

man's ability to actively interfere with his emotive process at the most tragic moment of his life. "Aaron," in the Rav's words, "withdrew from himself—he withdrew from being a father. This kind of movement of recoil is tantamount to self-denial. Such action is certainly cathartic because it is certainly heroic. As such it is far more exalted than the aesthetic catharsis in the Greek sense." We should add that maybe that is why those whose ears are attuned to biblical Hebrew will find it difficult to emotionally divorce themselves from the mysterious power that the two words *vayidom Aharon* project.

MOURNING RECOILS FROM THE SABBATH

The Rav resorts to a more easily identifiable example of dialectical catharsis: the head-on collision, as it were, between a person in mourning and the Sabbath day, when one is halakhically not supposed to mourn. "The mourner who has buried a beloved wife or a mother returns home from the cemetery where he has left part of himself, where he witnessed the mockery of human existence. He is in a mood to question our entire axiological universe. The house is empty. Every corner weeps with memories. Yet the Halakhah addresses itself to the lonely mourner and whispers to him: Rise from your mourning. Cast off the ashes from your head. Change your clothes; light the festive candles; recite the *Kiddush* over a cup of wine—a *Kiddush* extolling the Lord for having given us festivals of gladness and sacred seasons of joy. . . . Pronounce the blessing of *sheheḥeyanu,* 'Blessed are Thou, O Lord God, who has kept us in life and has preserved us and has enabled us to reach this season.'

"The Halakhah," the Rav explains, "which at times can be very tender, understanding, and accommodating, may, on other occasions, act like a disciplinarian, demanding obedience. . . . The Halakhah suggests to man, broken in body and spirit, carrying the burden of an absurd existence, that he change his mood, that he cast off his grief, and choose joy. . . . Is such a metamorphosis of the state of mind of an individual possible? Can one make the leap from utter black desolation and helplessness into joyous trust? Can one replace the experience of monstrosity with a feeling of the highest meaningfulness? I have no right to judge. However I know of people who attempted to perform this greatest of all miracles" ("Catharsis").[2]

The Rav also speaks of states of existentially necessary catharsis of religious life which consist in the awareness of long interludes during which man finds himself at an infinite distance from God. Here again the Rav resorts to the absurd: "On the long life journey, at one point or another, one must reach the absurd stage at which one finds himself bankrupt and forlorn. The Bible, with ruthless honesty, recorded experiences of failure [even] in the lives of our greatest. Man must be cognizant of this tragic fact, which sooner or later he must encounter, if his metaphysical destiny is to be realized." And here the Rav utters some exceedingly daring thoughts, exceeded only by their disarming honesty and valiant sense of truth: "Great is not the man who has never faltered, but the man who tripped, fell, and rose again to greater heights. . . . Sin is a reality, not just a potential threat.[3] Perfect man has never been created. If a man is not conscious of the contradiction inherent in the very core of his personality, he lives in the world of illusions and leads an unredeemed existence. It matters not that

---

2. So does the author, and may it be permitted to him to introduce what is more than a personal note: Whatever is truly exemplary goes beyond the personal. Nothing can make me forget the Sabbath table back home in Lithuania a couple of days after my father's death. My father, I should add, was a graduate of the Slobodka Yeshiva, a known *talmid ḥakham*, and for four years the *ḥavrutah* (study companion) of the Ḥazon Ish. There she sat, my saintly mother, who warned us, the children, against permitting our emotions to interfere with the sanctity of the Sabbath. It was well-nigh impossible for us children, who had just lost a young, truly adored father, not to show how we felt on the first Sabbath without him. Mother, however, noticing the tears in our eyes, exclaimed time and again: "Sabbath, children . . . Sabbath!" and that was enough. When the Sabbath was over, she passed out.

3. Sartre speaks of evil the way the Rav speaks of sin: "We have been taught to take evil seriously. It is neither our fault nor our merit that we lived at a time when torture was a daily fact. Chateaubriand, Ordour, the Rue de Saussais [a Nazi torture chamber], Dachau, and Auschwitz have all demonstrated to us that evil is not an appearance; that knowing its cause does not dispel it; that it is not opposed to good as a confused idea is to a clear one; that it is not the effect of passions that might be cured, or a feat which might be overcome; of a passing aberration which might be excused; of an ignorance which might be enlightened, and it can in no way be diverted, brought back, reduced, and incorporated into idealistic humanity like that shade of which Leibnitz has written that it is necessary for the glare of the light."

we call such a complacent state of mind—self-righteousness, pride, haughtiness, stupidity—it is all a manifestation of a brutish and raw state of mind."

To the Rav, one might say without fear of contradiction, a phrase like "peace of mind" would be not just a contradiction in terms, but an outright existential lie: it is *either peace or mind.* One cannot have both. The great Hasidic master Reb Mendel of Kotzk, whom the Rav does not mention anywhere, though they have much in common, may have been closest to the Rav's thought when he interpreted the passage in Proverbs "He who increases knowledge increases pain" to mean: "Increase your knowledge though it will increase your pain!"

Rabbi Nehemia Nobel, the inspired German Orthodox rabbi and teacher of Franz Rosenzweig, did speak of the possibility of a certain kind of inner peace when he interpreted in his own way the following passage (Isaiah 57:20–21): "But the wicked are like the troubled seas that cannot rest. . . . There is no peace, saith the Lord, to the wicked." To this Rabbi Nobel comments: "The Lord has shown great kindness to us sinners, whose souls were like the turbulent seas and who will know no peace until we return to Him in true repentance." Here peace of mind is not a "religious" promise at all. It is a redemptive hope.

FREEDOM AND THE PRINCIPLE OF REDEMPTIVE RETREAT

The Halakhah, according to the Rav, attributes extraordinary importance to the principle of retreat as a dialectical condition for ultimate advance! The retreat, in the Rav's view, assumes the nature not only of a religious paradigm, but of an existential *sine qua non.* We shall therefore be on safe ontological ground if we try to suggest that unless the halakhic principle of creative retreat is applied to freedom, we may face the danger of losing it. What we mean to say is that the halakhic law of timely retreat as applied to freedom of love may also apply to love of freedom. Exactly as there comes a moment when a person must place restraints on his freedom of love, there comes a point when man must place restraints on his love of freedom. Both in the first as in the second case, retreat must be voluntarily practiced so as to infuse the resumed advance, when the time is right, with greater passion and greater meaning. We can easily trace the law of the first retreat in the Bible. Where in the Torah do we find retreat applying to the love of freedom?

If the entire Halakhah, as the Rav maintains, consists of one great dialectical series of advances and retreats, and "both are the words of the living God" (Gittin 6), we may take the liberty of deducing, in the spirit of the Rav's teaching, a halakhic postulate from a biblical narrative. Biblical narratives are quite often treasure chests of laws. What we have in mind is the seemingly strange order given to Moses by the Lord God Yahveh that he go to Pharaoh and tell him, "Let My people go so that they may serve Me." There is a strange antinomy here: the Israelites are *avadim*, that is to say, "slaves" in Egypt. But Moses is not told by God to tell Pharaoh just to set the slaves free, but to free them so that they may serve Him, be His *avadim—veyaavduni—*in the wilderness! Wouldn't it have been much more logical, and much more exhilarating, if the Almighty had promised to give them what they most lacked in Egypt—freedom? But here we are dealing, it seems, with a dialectical stance of enormous proportions: by the very insertion in the call for freedom of one word, *veyaavduni* ("and they shall serve Me"), freedom was provided, as it were, with a built-in retreat formula. What is implied in this clarion call for true freedom is this: Freedom will be true to you as to Me if you will know *not to misuse it*, that is to say, if, by following My laws, you will know how and when to resist the allure of its misuse by a timely retreat.

There is something equally timely and timeless about this seeming antinomy. The sages commented on it, as mentioned in another chapter, in a most felicitous manner when they used the word *harut*, "engraved," to signify also *herut*, "freedom." "Don't read [that the law was] *harut* [engraved] upon the tablets, but *herut* [freedom]." That is to say, the "thou shalt" and the "thou shalt nots" of the law may seem to you to be interfering with your freedom, but they actually and ultimately *guarantee it.*

THE FREEDOM ONE SHOULD RETREAT FROM

At work now in the free world, as in the world which had just regained its freedom, are powerful forces dragging the life order in the direction of misusing freedom in the name of using it to the hilt. What happened is that the dialectic of the emancipatory process led into the transformation of freedom of thought into "free thought." But there is a world of difference here. Contrary to freedom of thought, which is an affirmation of man's creativity and responsibility, free thought is a denial of man's spiritual dimension. My glory may lie in the fact that I am free to sin, but even more so in my inner power to *refrain* from—to retreat—from sinning. This refraining, or retreating, is an idea which is simply missing from free thought. Nicholas Berdyaev, the distinguished Russian philosopher, writes: "By now we see how the autonomy of thought, which was proclaimed in all spheres of social, cultural, political, and religious life, has brought about the dissociation of these various phases of life from the integral man, from man in his hoped-for wholeness. . . . The crisis and decline of the freedom of thought is in direct causal relation with the fact that it is not so much man's thought which is set free, as that thought has been set free from man, has become autonomous. But this autonomy is something quite different from freedom" (*The Fate of Man*).

By now we know, after all the experience we have had, and are still having, with such organizations as, for example, the American Civil Liberties Union, that liberalism which is not mature enough to know when to retreat may actually find itself defending nihilism in the name of free thought. And this is inevitable. A liberty which is strictly formal and legalistic is bound to be indifferent to truth and, which is worse, *ignorant* of what human truth is all about. Civil libertarians who do not know how and when to make the movement of retreat from free thought are doomed to defend the worst in us in the name of the best in our tradition, like the terrifyingly misunderstood and misinterpreted First Amendment.

Free thought implies the common, the low, the plebeian. Using Kantian terminology, it might be said that the realm of nature is the realm of the animalistic in man. The fact that the realm of nature is what the adherents of free thought hold up like a banner anytime libertinism is attacked should suffice to brand it as an enemy of freedom of thought. The difference between freedom of thought and free thought is the same as that between freedom of love and free love: the first bespeaks the freedom inherent in the joy of true love; the other is clearly animalistic, or at best, hedonistic. The latter implies man devoid of any uniqueness, while the first implies personality. Personality, on its highest level, *is* freedom.

"But where do you draw the line?" the defendants of free thought ask, whenever they are told that we are sliding into nihilism. To this seemingly insurmountable question there is only one answer: It is not where we draw the line, but who draws it. Only sages can do it, not "experts," and they are a disappearing species, alas! So what can be done? Go back to the sages of old! "Life must be lived forward," Kierkegaard said, "but can be understood only backward." Goethe put it even more directly: "The truth was discovered long ago." A Hebrew sage and kabbalist of the nineteenth century, Elijah Benamozegh, spelled it out: "Antiquity is the most infallible sign of truth."

THE LONELY MAN OF FAITH

"Perfect man has never been created" is a follow-up on the thought, so essential to Judaism, as the Rav maintains, that "man was created to create himself." If the Creator has left a part of His creation imperfect, so that man could engage in the creative act, this actually means that the creative act, which was not completed by God, can never be completed, only advanced, by man. It also means that the creative act, since it cannot be completed, is exceedingly painful. It would be safe to assume that among those grandees of the soul whose effort at self-creation is greatest, the creative pain is the strongest. The Rav, a man of towering greatness of mind and soul, does not hesitate to speak very openly about his own encounters with despair. "I am lonely," the Rav says, (in "The Lonely Man of Faith"). "Let me emphasize, however, that by stating 'I am lonely' I do not intend to convey to you the impression that I am alone. I, thank God, do enjoy the love and friendship of man. I meet people, talk, argue, reason; I am surrounded by comrades and acquaintances. And yet, companionship and friendship do not alleviate the passionate experience of loneliness which drains me constantly. I am alone because at times I feel rejected and thrust away by everybody, not excluding my most intimate friends, and the words of the psalmist 'my father and my mother have forsaken me' quite often ring in my ears.''

An even more distressing admission of existential perplexity is expressed in the following lines (which appear in "Redemption, Prayer, Talmud Torah"): "I know that I am perplexed, that my fears are irrational, incoherent. At times I am given over to panic; I am afraid of death. At other times I am horrified at the thought of becoming, God forbid, incapacitated during my lifetime; I don't know what to fear, what not to fear. I am utterly confused and ignorant."

I came across a curious observation on the Rav's admission of dark spells in a book by a Conservative rabbi, Harold Schulweis, entitled *In God's Mirror.*

"Look," he asks, "if the Rav hasn't found an answer to his mental agonies, what are we to say to the American Jew who doesn't look for an answer to the question of what he can do for Judaism but of what Judaism can do for him?" "Don't tell me," the rabbi quotes the inquiring Jew, "what I am to do for the sake of the synagogue, for the sake of Zion, or for the sake of mitzvot. Tell me what Judaism can do for me. Tell me what the synagogue can do for me. Tell me what the Jewish community can do for me. Tell me what the mitzvot can do for me—for me not as a dues-paying member, not as an element of the collective set of a people, but for me, in my existential loneliness, in my despair and bore-dom, in my inability to collaborate, to laugh, or to cry."

He was right: they can do nothing for him!

The synagogue can do nothing for him, for in the Rav's words, as mentioned earlier, "It was not the synagogue, but the bet medrash—the house of study—which occupied the central place in Jewish life," and "house of study" meant exactly that: study! Had the Jew studied the Torah *lishma*, he would not have asked what the mitzvot can do for him, for he would have known first-hand what they can do *to* him. They would not have entirely alleviated his existential despair, but in moments of despair and boredom he would have known where to look for sparks of inspired guidance. The psalmist, who oscillates no less than the Rav between heights of joy and depths of despair, expresses it very succinctly when he says: "If Thy Torah were not my joy I would have been lost in my misery." The very declaration of love for the Torah is accompanied by an admission of a lurking misery dark enough to get lost in.

That is why Judaism can promise only one thing to a Jew who is asking such questions: an acquired ability, through many years of search, prayer, and study, to heroically "wrestle with God."

Judaism cannot make the Jew feel better about himself unless he reaches the high rung of realizing that he is, since Jacob's name became Israel, a God-wrestler. He must wrestle with God as a presence in matters pertaining to the law, and he must wrestle with Him as an "absence" in moments of existential despair. As the psalmist says, "You hid Your face and I am terrified" (Ps. 30:8). There is no such thing as a straight line between an enlarged understanding, that is to say, *Da'at Hashem*, and the constancy of feeling good about oneself. Aside from an enlarged understanding by means of *Da'at Hashem* there is an enlarged understanding by means of suffering. As the psalmist puts it, "Troubles have enlarged my heart" (Ps. 25:17). The Rav warns against the thought, which has become the mental and emotional snare of hundreds of thousands of Americans, many of them Jews, who are easy prey for all kinds of cults. Seduced by promises of quick psychic fixes and straight, short lines to "feeling good" about oneself, they even believe—and it is here where ignorance closes ranks with wishful thinking—that there is such a thing as transcendental meditation, for example, which can be acquired by means of an exercise, like bicycling or swimming—except that bicycling or swimming takes longer to learn!

"THE LORD IS MY SHEPHERD" AND "OUT OF THE DEPTHS"

"The Lord is my shepherd, I shall not want; He maketh me lie down in green pastures; He leadeth me beside the still waters" (Ps. 23). "This psalm," says the Rav, "only describes the ultimate destination of the homo religiosus, not the path leading to that destination. For the path that will eventually lead to 'the green pastures' and to 'the still waters' is not the royal road, but a narrow, twisting footway that threads its course along the steep mountain slope, as the terrible abyss yawns at the traveler's feet'' (''The Halakhic Man'').

It is of particular significance to note that the psalm just before the famous Twenty-third quoted above is one which is its very opposite. That is to say, a psalm that speaks of the extremes of pain, sorrow, and despair in life: ''I am poured out like water, and all my bones are out of joint. My heart has become like wax; it melts in the midst of my bowels. . . . My strength is dried up like a potsherd, and my tongue cleaveth to my jaws, and Thou has brought me down into the dust of death'' (Ps. 22:15–16).

The very proximity of the two psalms bears witness to the antinomy inherent, as the Rav teaches, in the Jewish way of thought. The Twenty-second Psalm is an admission of despair; the Twenty-third, a song of glory. How do we reconcile the opposites? We don't. Somewhere between the Twenty-second and Twenty-third Psalms there lies hidden the secret of God-wrestling as first experienced by Jacob when he wrestled through the mysterious night with a celestial being. What this comes to teach us is the great dialectical truth that human creativity is induced by the Divine will that man wrestle with Him. Wrestling with God, in the biblical sense, does not mean rebellion, but standing up to him. That was the Kotzker's interpretation of the passage ''When its waves rise, You praise them'' (Ps. 89:10).

The entire idea that the schism in human nature which runs through the human personality at every level is due to man's revolt against his Maker, as Christian theology has preached since the days of Augustine, is, as the Rav sees it, foreign to Judaism. ''Unlike this view, according to which it was man who, by his sinful rebellion against his Maker, precipitated the split in human nature, the Judaic view posits that the schism is willed by God as a source of man's greatness and his election as a singular charismatic being. . . . Man is a great and creative being because he is torn by conflict and is always in a state of ontological tenseness and perplexity. The fact that the creative gesture is associated with agony is a result of this contradiction which prevades the whole personality of man'' (''Majesty and Humility'').[4]

---

4. Gustave Mahler said in a letter to a friend written after the Munich Orchestra refused

The idea that "the creative gesture is associated with agony" is to the Rav essential to man's understanding of his existential status. Unlike the abstract Hegelian dialectic, the dialectic of Judaism is "irreconcilable and hence interminable." What is meant by this is that Judaism accepted a dialectic consisting only of thesis and antithesis. The third Hegelian stage, the Rav avers, that of synthesis, or reconciliation, is missing. "The conflict is final and almost absolute. Only God knows how to reconcile; we don't. Complete reconciliation is an eschatological—messianic—vision. To Hegel, man and his history were just abstract ideas. In the world of abstraction, synthesis is possible. To Judaism," the Rav concludes, in words which are existentialist to the hilt, "man has always been and still is, a living reality or, may I say, a tragic living reality. In the world of realities the harmony of opposites is an impossibility."

The question, of course, arises whether the Halakhah, the life blood of Judaism—replete as it is with theses and antitheses—does not offer endless occasions for synthesis. And we do not mean the synthesis between various disputations concerning one law or another, but the great existential and ontological synthesis in man brought about by the very process of his creative "dialogue" with the Halakhah as a whole. In other words, doesn't the *experienced* Halakhah heal the rift between life and the spirit?

The Rav is somehow vague in his answer. Juxtaposing two famous biblical passages "What is man that Thou are mindful of him, the son of man that Thou thinkest of him?" and "Yet Thou hast made him but a little lower than the angels," etc., the Rav says that "the homo religiosus has yet to find the third harmonizing verse" (between the two seemingly contradictory ones). "However," he asserts, "halakhic man *has* found the third verse—the Halakhah! He too suffers from this dualism, from this deep spiritual split, but he mends the split through the concept of Halakhah and law."

What does the Rav mean by "mending the split"? It is the conviction of this author that the Rav had in mind the experience of cognitive firmness which the Halakhah provides the halakhic

---

him the conductor's baton that he now understood why, as was the case with Patriarch Jacob, creativity must be paid for with a wound.

man in the very midst of a dreadfully unfirm and unstable existence. When the halakhic man finally grasps the *Grandezza* of Halakhah, he comes to it only after he has gone through the dark backstreets of unpaved, muddy areas which he had threaded. Once he is within the domain of Halakhah, however, he will never go astray in the blind alleys and narrow pathways of the world's emptiness and chaos. "All stands before him beautifully finished and adorned. . . . Halakhic man is a man of the law and the principle, a man of the statute and the judgment, and therefore he always possesses his being, even if at times it should be afflicted with deep melancholy, a fixed, firm, Archimedean point that is outside and above the turbulence of his soul, beyond the maelstrom of the effective life, a true source of peace and tranquility" ("Halakhic Man").

A true source (but only a source) of peace and tranquility because it is an experiential source of truth. The consciousness of a lived truth is a source of peace and tranquility because it testifies to an authenticity that bears the stamp of eternity. The Rav's placing the halakhic man way above the homo religiosus is precisely because authenticity to the Rav means a normative a priori mode of dealing with the whole man in his entire earthly existence, while the homo religiosus is trying to transcend that existence by overpreoccupation with his soul. The halakhic man often substitutes retreat for transcendence: "The halakhic man does not quiver before any man; he does not seek out compliments, nor does he require public approval. If he sees that there are fewer and fewer men of distinguished spiritual rank about, then he wraps himself up in his mantle and hides away in the four cubits of Halakhah. He knows that the truth is a lamp unto his feet and the Halakhah a light unto his path. His whole being loathes idlers, wastrels, and loafers. Piety that is not based upon knowledge of the Torah is of no consequence in his view. There can be no fear of God without knowledge and no service of God without the cognition of halakhic truth. 'A crude man fears no sin, nor is a man ignorant of the Torah pious' (Avot 2:5). The old saying of Socrates that virtue is knowledge is strikingly similar to the stance of halakhic man" ("The Halakhic Man").

What all this means is that halakhic man is, as it were, allergic to inauthenticity. And inauthenticity to him is not necessarily a premeditated hypocrisy, but quite often a lack of awareness of what existential and ontological needs are all about. The Rav stresses this unawareness to the maximum when he does not hesitate to point out that in our unawareness of our inner needs, we may not even know that we constantly deceive ourselves; that we live a lie from which we do not retreat because we do not know it is a lie. This lie, as the Rav puts it, may even appear at times a "a moral lie"!

We shall have more to say about this in the next chapter.

4

Self-Creation, Self-Deception, and Need-Awareness

IT IS TORN MAN WHO IS THE CREATOR

A good part of the Rav's lectures on *teshuvah*, some of them lasting for three or four hours at a stretch, and delivered before ever-growing audiences of people caught up in the world of thought, were edited, translated, and published in English by the late Prof. Pinhas Peli. In his preface to "On Repentance," he points out that the fact that many hundreds of thinking people were spellbound by the Rav's presentation and interpretation of the laws concerning *teshuvah* bears testimony to their existential impact as much as to their religious significance. Only one part of the Rav's seminal work on repentance deals with the a-prioristic laws of *teshuvah* as codified mainly by Maimonides, from whom he rarely departs. Another part of the book deals with the a-posteriori consequences of consciously or unconsciously neglecting or rejecting it.

The law, in general, as the Rav sees it, is the highway to existential, not just religious, authenticity. This thought is basic to the Rav's world-view. Authenticity, however, does not necessarily mean completeness, but confrontation (of which we spoke in a previous chapter). The wholehearted embracing of the law does not spell out the end of the inner struggle, but its elevation to a higher plateau of cognition. No self-deception here. The enemy from within is recognized as a source of pollution, for sin is not only transgression but, at bottom, a sickness. This sickness, however, is not entirely curable. Nor should it be. One may learn how

76

to treat it, not how to eradicate it. There is, moreover, a passion in sin which can be applied to good deeds and serve as a gateway to *teshuvah*. Nowhere in the Torah or in the sages is it said that sin can or should be completely suppressed, conquered, eliminated. The Almighty does not tell Cain, just before he kills his brother, that the evil urge in him can or must be destroyed. Very far from it. He tells him that "sin lieth at the door, and to you is his desire, and you shall rule over him."

The Divine demand here is to contain sin, not to eliminate it. Nor could it have been otherwise. If sin were eradicated, there would have been no freedom of choice and no creativity in the world. When the Rav rejects most emphatically the Christian overemphasis on "original sin," he addresses himself to the essence of the human condition, namely free will. Of course, this implies a state of duality in human nature, but to the Rav, as to other grandees of Halakhah, it seems to be a foregone conclusion that the duality in human nature is part of man's tragic but heroic destiny, and, at the same time, the secret of his creativity. Both these axiological human distinctions emanate precisely from the tension generated by the inevitable clash between the two opposing poles of gravity and grace.

The Rav's insistence on the nonredeemable nature of the inner split in man is so categorical that he regards it as a curse and a blessing which are, as it were, in constant need of each other. Sin is a curse, but one could not, without sin, achieve the heroic stance of recoiling from sin. Hence sin is a necessary curse. Thus, the Rav regards sin as equally indispensable and intolerable. It is this horrendous dichotomy which the Rav dares call a "moral lie." Moral lie? Yes, a moral lie! "Moral" because out of this crucible there have emerged some extraordinarily creative and purified souls. "Lie" because this emergence would be well-nigh impossible without the awareness, and the experience, of gravity as the lie which drags us down, but without which the lifting up of creative tension would be impossible!

AND I SAID IN MY HASTE, ALL MEN ARE LIARS

"What kind of lie did the psalmist have in mind when he hurled this serious accusation at man in general?" the Rav asks (in

"Majesty and Humility"). "Did he have in mind the lie which the 'I' tells the 'Thou'? Did he refer to the everyday social lie? Did he refer to the commercial lie of the dishonest businessman, to the political lie of the faithless ruler, to the judicial lie of the perjurer? In a word, did he speak of the profitable, immoral lie? Does man indeed engage constantly in immoral lying? By no means! The psalmist is concerned with a different kind of lie: the existential lie that man tells not others but himself. Man is indeed a liar, because he is involved in an unresolvable contradiction, in an insoluble dialectic, because he is caught, like Abraham's ram, in a thicket of antinomies and dichotomies. He swings like a pendulum between two poles: the thesis and the antithesis, the affirmation and the negation, identifying himself either with both or with neither. He must lie, but this inevitable lie is rooted in man's uniqueness and is a *moral lie*. It is the wellspring of human creativity. That agony accompanies the process of creativity is due to the fact that it is *torn* man who is the creator" ("Catharsis").

The Rav explains what he meant by a moral lie: since dialectical man cannot be committed to a uniform, homogeneous reality, his moral gesture, too, is bound to be ambiguous. Man, captive, as he is, of two enchanting but contradictory visions, is inevitably attracted by two sets of values: "Two stars, infinitely distant from each other, beckon to him." Man must decide which star to follow, and in his indecision he is not an immoral man, but a confused man. "Man, confused, kneels in prayer, petitioning God, who has burdened him with this dialectic, to guide him and to enlighten him." What kind of enlightenment is he praying for? The enlightenment that is required to reach a state in which he is no longer mistaken about his real needs. Does this mean total redemption? Not even the Halakhah promises such a state. "The Halakhah is, of course, concerned with this dilemma and tries to help man in such critical moments." But even the Halakhah "did not discover the synthesis, since the latter does not exist. It did, however, find a way to enable man to respond to both calls" ("Majesty and Humility").

THE ENERGY OF SIN PULLS UPWARD

"To respond to both calls," that is to say, to gravity and grace simultaneously, can only be understood in the context of an extraordinary talmudic passage which speaks of the high rung—maybe the highest—which man can reach if he serves his Maker "with both urges," the good and the bad. A great deal of commentary has been expended on this enigmatic passage, but its meaning, so it seems to this author, can be grasped by a bold thought which, strange as it may sound, is common to the Rav and to Friedrich Nietzsche, for whom the Rav has little sympathy. Nietzsche thought that the power of what is right can gain the upper hand only if "infused with the energy generated by murder." That is, of course, an energy too terrifying to contemplate. The Rav, however, without any reference to Nietszche, says something which is not dissimilar in essence: "The energy of sin pulls, as it were, upward."

"The energy of sin pulls upward," but only if the downward energy which preceded it was, as it were, as good as irresistible. The Rav goes even further in this daring direction and reaches some truly startling conclusions: "When one reaches the exalted level of elevating evil, one can no longer say, 'And this is my acquittal'; one can no longer say, 'I have brought my sacrifice; I have made a break with the past, and now I am a different person.' No, I am *not* a different person. I am *not* starting anew. I am continuing *onward*. I am sanctifying evil and raising it to new heights."

These are mighty words and, which is as important, mighty thoughts. The dialectical sweep of the Rav's perception of *teshuvah* here reaches unequaled heights. In the light of this razor-sharp insight, it should not be difficult to understand the deeper reason for the famous saying by the sages that "not even the truly righteous can stand where the truly penitent stand." The truly penitent, the truly great, create or *recreate* their Divine creatureliness by reestablishing their claim to the *tzelem*.

THE TALMID ḤAKHAM AS THE VISIBLE PERSONIFICATION OF THE TZELEM

The *talmid ḥakham*, the halakhic man, is to the Rav the *visible* personification of the *tzelem*. And I stress "visible," for the *tzelem*, to the Rav, is a proposition of *completeness*. When the Rav speaks of the halakhic man, he time and again draws a distinction between the halakhic man and the homo religiosus, who quite often wears his religiosity like a garment, and even like a neglected one. It is enough to read what the Rav has to say about his late uncle, the revered Gaon and Tzadik, Reb "Velvele"—Yitzhak Zeev—Soloveichik, in order to understand why it took "marriage to the Torah," as the Rav puts it, speaking of Reb Velvele, for him to complete his *tzelem Elokim*. Reb Yitzhak Zeev, in the Rav's words, was not just "living *with* the Torah"—that would have meant being "engaged" to Torah—but living *it*. In a eulogy surpassing all imperfect offices of praise and grace, the Rav, using the most endearing and edifying metaphors from the Song of Songs, where the word *dodi*, "my uncle," is used to signify "my beloved," grapples with the question of "why is my beloved more than another beloved?" and comes up with elucidations of what it means to be "married to the Torah," to be "it" instead of being "with it," which raises them to heights of poetry at its most sublime:

> Rapt into still communion that transcends
> The imperfect offices of prayer and praise,
> His mind was a thanksgiving to the power
> That made him; it was blessedness and love.

It has been remarked that Wordsworth, the great English poet, is by no means saying, in the last two lines, that this exalted human being was giving thanks, that he knew himself blessed, that he felt himself loving or loved. He is saying that he himself, his whole being, *was* blessedness. He was "rapt"; he was merged. Subject and object had become one.

"MY BELOVED IS WHITE AND RUDDY"

Here is another quotation from the Song of Songs which the Rav invokes as symbolically descriptive of his uncle: "My beloved [*dodi*] is white and ruddy, the chiefest among ten thousand." Here the "beloved" is described, as it were, in "colors": "white and ruddy." "Like the sight of the rainbow in the clouds, so is the vision of Divine honor projected in the personalities of the great men of Israel. . . . Out of the depths of their souls shines forth a wondrous light which explodes into a myriad of colors. . . . The greatness of such people bursts forth from them with an extraordinary power to faraway distances and it is all-conquering. It is visible to all. Even the simple and the coarse, the ignoramus and the man of the street are powerless to resist them'' (''Why Is My Beloved More Than Another Beloved?'')

''My beloved is white and ruddy, chiefest among the ten thousand.'' The truth of the matter is that even if there is only one *talmid ḥakham* among ten thousand who is a witness to the truth of the *tzelem*, the halakhic man has made his point. And his point is unmistakable: understanding as a mode of being in the world.

This can only be said about the halakhic man, not about the homo religiosus. We continually get the impression that the Rav, in his repeated attempts to define the distinction between the halakhic man and the homo religiosus, was trying to ward off the danger of the *talmid ḥakham*'s countenance being blurred by pious ignoramuses who masquerade as *talmidei ḥakhamim*.

HOMO RELIGIOSUS AND HALAKHIC MAN

''Contrary to the homo religiosus,'' the Rav writes, ''halakhic man is firmly embedded in this world and does not suffer from the pangs of dualism of the spiritual and the corporeal, of the soul which ascends on high and the body which descends below. We do not have here a person who strains against the chains of the ethical and the rein of the norm and accepts them against his will. Rather, we have here a blending of the obligation with self-consciousness, a merging of the norm with the individual, and a union of the outside command with the inner will and conscience of man'' (''The Halakhic Man'').

The last assertion is, of course, a clear reference to the Kantian insistence that adherence to ''statutes imposed from without'' is untenable on the grounds of moral autonomy. As the Rav sees it— that is to say, as the Torah sees it—however, the so-called ''outside'' of the law becomes the whole-life content of the Torah insider.

But the Rav goes on to say that unlike the Christian saints, whose lives consisted of a long series of battles with the dazzling allure of life, with carnal, this-worldly pleasures, "the great Jewish scholars knew nothing about man's conflict with the evil urge. The church fathers devoted themselves to religious life in a state of compulsion and duress; the Jewish sages, in a state of joy and freedom" ("The Halakhic Man").

How is one to understand the statement that "the great Jewish scholars knew nothing about man's conflicts with the evil urge" when a thousand passages in the Talmud and Midrash can easily attest to the contrary? How can one understand such a statement, moreover, in view of the Rav's own words about his own inner struggles, his dark moments, totally devoid of "joy and freedom," but replete with fear and trembling about the tornness in his own self? To this we can offer only one answer: the conflict with the evil urge is one thing, the struggle with dark spells is another. There is the badness of dark spells, and there are the dark spells of badness, and they are not the same. Patriarch Jacob, whose seemingly absurd wrestling with a supernal being the Rav regards as the epitome of tragic heroism; Jacob, to whom God has revealed Himself and to whom He has promised grace and protection—why did he tremble and fear in the night he was left alone with Esau in his pursuit? Because no amount of faith immunizes one against the dark spells of fear and doubt. The halakhic man is not immune to it either. But "the halakhic man always possesses in his being, even if at times it should be afflicted with deep melancholy, a fixed, firm, Archimedean point that is outside and above the turbulence of his soul" ("The Halakhic Man").

One can say, it seems, that the ontological, non-normative thoughts of great-souled men are like the Psalms or the Book of Ecclesiastes—subject to the fierce sways of moodiness. The psalmist confesses that "when my spirit faints within me, You know my path [i.e., You know what is taking place in me]: on the road that I walk they have laid a snare for me. Looking to the right I see that I have no friend; every escape is lost to me, no one seeks to save my life. I have cried out to You, O Lord, 'You are my refuge, my portion in the land of the living.' Attend my cry, for I have been brought very low," etc. If there is a radical change of mood in the psalmist, it is not due to an inner dualism but to a Jobean perplexity about God's ways with man. What is unchangeable in the Rav's thought, as in the teachings of Judaism, is the paramount idea that the Torah is the road to holiness. However, contrary to any kind of facile mysticism, the Rav stresses that the road in question, though a lifelong labor of love and joy, is interspersed with fear and trembling, and requires a lifetime of effortful pursuit—the only pursuit of which it can be said that it is, or may evolve into, in the purest spiritual sense, a pursuit of happiness. "Man does not become holy through mystical adhesion to the absolute nor through mysterious union with the Infinite, nor through boundless, all-embracing ecstasy; but rather through his whole biological life, through his animal actions, and through actualizing the Halakhah in the empirical world" ("The Halakhic Man").

TO BRING GOD DOWN TO EARTH

The Halakhah, to the Rav, is a Divine blueprint endowing man with the power and authority, as it were, "to bring God down to earth." To follow this blueprint is the road to holiness, for "the Halakhah denotes *the appearance of a mysterious transcendence in the midst of our concrete world.*" Mysticism is not treated lightly here, but the halakhic existentialism transcends it, for it does not just accommodate a great yearning, but it encompasses the whole man in the reality of his daily life. "Holiness does not wink at us from 'beyond' like some mysterious star that sparkles in the distant heavens, but appears in our actual, very real lives."

The Rav's descriptions of the men who merit the appearance of holiness in their "very real lives" are of exalted human beings who vindicate the opinions of other giants of Halakhah, like the Hazon Ish of our day and age, who speaks of the angelic status of men who reach the stage of knowing the Torah: "And in fact, he who merits the knowing of the Torah (that is to say, that the lower reason, which is implanted in the *nefesh* like a seed in the ground, merged with wisdom and became one), may walk amongst people and seem to people who judge only by seeing, as a man, while he is, in truth, an angel who lives with mortals, but it is a life of nobility, elevated above all praise and glory" (*Letters*, 13).

If we bear in mind that *nefesh* is the animal soul in man, always on a collision course with wisdom, which resides in the *ru'ah* and *neshamah*, we see what the Ḥazon Ish had in mind: a man can reach the rung of the angels when a synthesis takes place in him between gravity and grace, between the *nefesh* and the *ru'aḥ*. A synthesis is, in other words, possible.

MAN RESIDES TOGETHER WITH HIS CREATOR IN THIS WORLD

The Rav himself, who emphasized on various occasions the seeming irreconcilability of the spiritual (wisdom) with the corporeal (*nefesh*), seems to see it differently. In "The Halakhic Man" he relates a story he was told by Reb Simha Zelig, the disciple and friend of his grandfather, Reb Haim. Once the two of them visited the house of a learned friend in Vilna, and while they were waiting for him, Reb Haim glanced through some works of Ḥabad Hasidism that were lying on the table. The books, which discussed the motivation of the Creator in creating the world, cited two opinions: (1) God created the world for the sake of His goodness; (2) He created it for the sake of His grace. Reb Haim turned to his friend and said: "Both views are incorrect. The world was created neither for the sake of His goodness nor for the sake of His grace, *but for the sake of His will.*"

Attention should be paid to the subtlety of the argument. Neither in the first opinion nor in the second does it say that the world was created *by* His goodness or *by* His will; this is taken for granted. The difference consists of the purpose, not of the cause. When Reb Haim insists that the world was created "for the sake of His will," he actually means that creation was conceived by the Creator as a process of a *continuous unfolding* of His will *in* and *by* His obedient creatures.

The Rav remarks that this view, set down by Maimonides as a firm principle in the *Guide* and prevalent in many forms in voluntaristic religion and metaphysical systems (e.g., Solomon Ibn Gabirol in *Mekor Ḥayyim* and that of Duns Scotus, who was influenced by the former) "is the very seal of halakhic man. The world was created in accordance with the will of God, who wills to 'contract' His Divine Presence in it. Therefore we are called upon to act and arrange our lives in accordance with this fundamental idea." This fundamental idea, we should add, the idea that the world was created for the sake of His will, clearly implies that His will, for the sake of which the world was created, must express itself in a divinely inspired blueprint available to man and aimed at telling him how to go about complying with it. Judaism claims that this blueprint is the Torah, which is the constitution of the Kingdom of God on earth in the making. "In its ideal shape and limit," Leon Roth writes (in *Judaism: a Portrait*), "Judaism may be looked upon as the concern with citizenship in the Kingdom of God. We must now note that one of the characteristics of this Kingdom, according to the view of Judaism, is that it has a written constitution."

And since this constitution is the Torah, and the Torah was given to man "to live by," the Rav rejects the mystical notion of a religious life which expresses itself in blind, misty, and even ecstatic gropings toward the great Unknown. Nor does he share the mystic's anguish, so prevalent in Hasidic and some kabbalistic literature, of *Shekhinta begalutah* ("The exile of His Presence"). To the Rav, the Divine Presence is present *in the Torah*. Of course, we are aware of the unfathomable grandeur of the ineffable *Deus absconditus*—God who conceals Himself in His dazzling hiddenness—"lofty and exalted, abiding in His heaven" (from a *piyyut* recited on the High Holy Days); but that very hiddenness can be experienced as revealedness in the midst of the cosmos by means of the Torah. "Halakhic man declares that the true home of the Divine Presence is in *this* world. The Divine Presence goes into exile, according to the opinion of halakhic man, when it departs from this world to the hidden and awesome transcendental realm." The world-to-come thus begins right here. Man brings to the afterlife the soul he refined by ethico-halakhic means throughout his entire life. The Zohar says that man wears in eternity the clothes he has woven for himself for a lifetime. Rabbi Haim of Volozhin builds on it his mystical psychology.

WHOLENESS AND HOLINESS

While such thoughts may have been hinted at by other exegetes, the Rav spelled it out with the authority and force of a learned conviction rarely matched before. His is, one may say without hesitation, the most existential interpretation of Judaism ever attempted, for it encompasses the whole man in a reality whose ideal is, indeed, experienced wholeness. Wholeness to the Rav is the equivalent of holiness.

Not only that "holiness is created by man, by flesh and blood," but "it is man who sanctifies place and makes a sanctuary for his Creator." The Rav explains this vital notion of Divine "contraction" by quoting a Midrash. "When God said to Moses, 'And let them make Me a sanctuary' (Exod. 25:8), Moses began to wonder, and he said, 'The glory of the Holy One, blessed be He, fills the upper world and the lower worlds, and yet He says, "And let them make Me a sanctuary"'! And, moreover, he gazed into the future and saw Solomon upon the completion of the building of the Temple, which was larger than the sanctuary, saying to the Holy One, blessed be He: 'But will God in very truth dwell on the earth? Behold, the heaven and the heaven of heavens cannot contain Thee; how much less the house that I have built' (I Kings 8:27). Therefore, Moses began to compose the psalm, 'The Most High dwelleth in concealment; the Almighty abideth in deep darkness' [Ps. 91]. God replied: 'I am not of the same opinion as you. But twenty boards in the north and twenty in the south and eight in the west [will suffice]. And more than that, I will contract My Divine Presence [so that it may dwell] in one square cubit' (Exodus Rabbah 34:1)" ("The Halakhic Man").

The Rav warns time and again that the mystery of *tzimtzum*, or "contraction," in the Halakhah does not touch upon questions of cosmogony, nor should one compare the concept of *tzimtzum* in the Halakhah with the concept as it appears in mystical doctrine. It is not only that "the ideal of the halakhic man is that the Divine Presence should rest here, in this world" but, as the Rav explains with unmatched dramatic vigor, the ideal halakhic man bears testimony to the actual presence of the divine in this world! And this applies not only to the highest stages of prophecy, as we learn in Judges 13:6, where a woman, a simple woman, Manoah's ignorant wife, described the godly man she had just seen as one whose "countenance was like that of an angel of God, most awesome," but that "the true Torah giants, the halakhic men par excellence . . . glow with a resplendent ethical beauty. . . . Holiness glows forth from every nuance of the personality, from every angle of its creative reality—from everything flows a special charm, a beauty that is not of this world, and is something wondrous and unique in every way.'' The Rav speaks in a noble poetic vein of the exalted state of the Torah sages down the ages, something that was always known to their contemporaries, but which people tend to overlook. But when truth is discussed as the main feature of the *tzelem*, it is also known among those who seek knowledge that that feature can be almost visible to the eye. ''The outpouring of their inner light is irresistible. . . . The countenance of the *talmid hakham* testifies to a strength of mind and a spiritual stature that sheds its brilliant light near and far, his whole being is imbued with the dignity of uniqueness and individuality, and displays a distinct streak of aristocracy'' (''The Halakhic Man'').

The almost inevitable ''moral lie'' has been as good as overcome here. Here we deal with witnesses to the truth. To Kierkegaard, a witness to the truth had to be a martyr. In Judaism, a witness to the truth is the upholder par excellence of a Torah of Life.

THE IMMORAL TRUTH

''Confronted man,'' as the Rav calls it, is aware of the ''moral lie'' which he is compelled to live or, at least, to face. But there is also such a thing as an ''immoral truth'' of which man is hardly aware, for he slips into it, as Sartre puts it, as into sleep, unconsciously. We are dealing here with the curse of self-deception, which has assumed epidemic proportions in our time, but which very few treat as a sickness, and even if they do they will not admit to it, for the life order demands that this sickness not be recognized for what it is.

The Rav speaks a great deal about self-deception, which man resorts to unconsciously so as to function in a life order which makes it increasingly difficult for him to know his own needs. As the Rav sees it, the biblical account of the creation of man portrays him, as explained in the second chapter, on three progressive levels. On the first level, man appears as a simple natural being. He is neither cognizant of his unique station in the cosmos nor burdened by the awareness of his paradoxical capability of being concurrently free and obedient. At this level, natural man is unresponsive to the pressure of both the imperative from without and the "ought" from within. "For the norm, either from within or from without, addresses itself only to man who is sensitive to his own incongruity and tragic dilemma." Natural man knows nothing of it.

When the Rav calls this man "natural man," he has in mind not the *urmensch* of bygone times, but modern man, whom he characterizes, as mentioned in another chapter, as a "nonconfronted man." According to the Rav, "nonconfronted man is to be found not only in the cave or in the jungle, but also in the seats of learning and in the halls of philosophers and artists. Nonconfrontation is not necessarily restricted to a primitive existence, but applies to human existence at all times, no matter how cultured and sophisticated" ("Confrontation").

A nonconfronted man, in other words, is neither conscious of his assignment vis-à-vis something which is outside of himself nor aware of his existential otherness, which is, in the final account, a summons by his Creator "to rise to tragic and heroic greatness."

Not enough attention has been paid to the Rav's insistence that nonconfrontation can easily go hand-in-hand with culture and sophistication. The Rav here actually addresses himself to a malaise which has now assumed epidemic proportions, but which very few dare to recognize for what it is. It is prevalent "in the seats of learning and in the halls of philosophers," but one can find its victims also in congregations and synagogues of various denominations. A Jew can be an intellectual and an *am ha'aretz* at the same time, but he can also be, at the same time, an *am ha'aretz* and a homo religiosus.

The question arises, as one reads the Rav's symptomatology of the homo religiosus, why he depicted as its prototype the "poetic" homo religiosus, the mystic, and hardly touched upon the "prosaic" one whom Maimonides, for example—Maimonides, whom the Rav rarely lets out of his sight—described in his famous parable about the King's Palace (*Guide* 3:51) as unworthy of entering the King's Palace. "Those who desire to arrive at the palace and enter it, but have never yet seen it, are the mass of religious people; the multitude that observe the Divine commandments, but are ignorant."

The Rav does not mention this all-too-familiar kind of homo religiosus, an omission which may be due, in our opinion, to the enormous difficulty one encounters in defining the various kinds of homo religiosus. The famous adage of the ages that "an *am ha'aretz* cannot be a righteous man" (a Hasid) does not necessarily apply to those among the unlearned and untutored who, in their moving simplicity and contriteness of heart, are painfully aware of their ignorance and are desperately trying to fill the void by prayer and good deeds. Such *amei ha'aretz* can be, in fact, fully confronted men. For to confront one's nothingness is already a reaching out toward a "somethingness," so to speak. And one can confront it in various ways and degrees.

Paul Tillich addresses himself to the question of confrontation in his own way, with which, however, every existential thinker will find common ground. "Look at the student," he writes (in *The Shaking of the Foundations*), "who knows the contents of the hundred most important books of world history, and yet whose spiritual life remains as shallow as it ever was, or perhaps becomes even more superficial. And then look at an uneducated worker who performs a mechanical task day by day, but who suddenly asks himself: 'What does it *mean* that I do this work? What does it mean for my life? What is the *meaning* of my life?' Because he asks these questions, this man is on the way into depth, whereas the other man, the student of history, dwells on the surface among petrified bodies, brought out from the depth by some spiritual earthquake of the past. The simple worker may grasp truth, even though he cannot answer his questions. The learned scholar may possess no truth even though he knows all the truths of the past."

The reason for this is that the product of scientific thought has been purged of its personal characteristics. Science, in other words, derives from a kind of knowing that has eliminated all the elements of the knower's personality. This means, in Paul Tillich's interpretation of the man who discovers ontological needs, that he must follow them and seek their answers in theology or philosophy. And it is here where Judaism begs to differ. The Torah, in the Rav's interpretation, in its only interpretation, is neither theology nor philosophy but *theonomy*. The answer to the question of

"What is the meaning of my life?" is provided by the relentless study of the Torah, by means of which impersonal law mysteriously acquires the power of a life content. This will never be understood by the despiritualized Jewish intellectual who can easily be an intellect and an *am ha'aretz* at the same time. As such, and his kind is legion, he is the nonconfronted man par excellence.

THE RISE OF THE INTELLECTUAL AM HA'ARETZ

It has been said that the Jewish intellectual is a doubly alienated creature: alienated as an intellectual and as a Jew. We can say, by the same token, that the nonconfronted Jewish intellectual is doubly nonconfronted: nonconfronted as a person and nonconfronted as a Jew.

Only in Judaism is such a phenomenon as an intellectual *am ha'aretz* possible. It has no equivalent in any other religion. The *am ha'aretz* is by no means the same as what is generally understood as an ignoramus. It is not the generality of ignorance we are talking about, but the ignorance of something in particular, the Torah. The intellectual *am ha'aretz,* because he is an intellectual, uses his ignorance of the Torah to attack it with all the eloquence and sharpness of an accomplished "man of his times." But that man was known in other times, too. The aggressively intellectual *am ha'aretz* whose kind is now rampant in Israel appeared on the Jewish scene millennia ago. There are passages in the Talmud which portray the *am ha'aretz* as exceedingly aggressive and self-confident in his enmity toward the *talmid hakham.* Reading what the sages had to say about this hatred, one cannot but conclude that we are dealing here not with a common ignoramus but with an *ideological am ha'aretz*—a loquacious opponent of Torah Judaism whose kind was rampant in the tannaic period no less than it is today. Rabbi Akiba, who up to his fortieth year was himself an *am ha'aretz*, goes so far as to portray him as a potential assassin. The Rav, in his memorable eulogy on his friend R. Haim Heller, speaks of the movement of the *minim* ("heretics") after the destruction of the Second Temple as of an internal enemy which was on relentless offensive "against tradition and against the continuous existence of the people as a separate entity."

The *amei ha'aretz*, like the *minim*, were thus ideological enemies, that is to say, intellectual *amei ha'aretz*, the most dangerous kind of *am ha'aretz*. And here we come again to the difference, in contemporary terms, between Jewish and non-Jewish intellectuals. Not much is demanded by way of religion, let alone learning, from a religious Christian intellectual. A profession of faith and a vague familiarity with theology are enough for him to qualify as a Christian. But for a Jewish intellectual *am ha'aretz* to present himself as a partner in any discussion of Judaism is intellectually dishonest and spiritually offensive.

The Rav uses some very bitter words in speaking about the abnormal phenomenon of Jewish intellectual *amei ha'aretz* from both sides of the ocean getting together in Israel to conduct dialogues about Jewishness. The Rav touches upon this aberration in his great essay about his uncle, Reb Zeev Soloveichik, and his attitude to Zionism. If Zionism, he says, expresses itself, among other things, in dialogues, organized by major Jewish organizations, between American Jewish writers appallingly ignorant of Judaism and Israeli literati adept at unleashing well-rounded phrases of contempt and abuse on everything that is sacred to Judaism, if this is Zionism, then his uncle was not a Zionist. The very idea that with the advent of the State of Israel, Jews no longer need to confront themselves as Jews, reeks, as the Rav sees it, of a fake universality which ends up in imitating not the best, but the worst in others. The dialectics of theonomy thus points simultaneously in two opposite directions; in the direction of an intimate relationship between the minutest detail of the law and "I am the Lord," on the one side, and, on the other, the intimate relationship between the professed universality of the intellectual *am ha'aretz* and his ontological mediocrity.

MEDIOCRITY AND UNIVERSALITY

The terms which the Rav uses to denote nonconfronted man, namely, "natural" and "universal," may be misunderstood. But what the Rav is trying to say with these characterizations is that nonconfronted man is, like nature or the universe, a "something in general." Man, the "second-rate man," as Berdyaev would call the person who ejected himself into the exterior, quite often loves to use the great universalist argument to prove his "progressiveness." In actuality, however, as the Rav sees it, there is something irremediably primitive about him, for he exists only by virtue of the species, that is to say, by virtue of the fact that he was born a member of the species and its general form is engraved upon him. He exists solely on account of his participation in the idea of the universal. He is just a member of the species man, an image of the universal. "He is just one more example of the species' image in its ongoing morphological process (in the Aristotelian sense of the term). He himself, however, has never done anything that could serve to legitimize his existence as an individual. His soul, his spirit, his entire being are grounded in the realm of the universal. [Hence] his roots lie deep in the soil of faceless mediocrity" ("The Halakhic Man").

THE RANDOM EXAMPLE OF THE BIOLOGICAL SPECIES

The Rav's treatment of mediocrity is unmerciful. Nor is he the only great existentialist thinker to react in this manner to a society which does not even realize that ingenuity, for example, has simply outrun intelligence. Today we know that there can be giants of ingenuity who are spiritual and existential dwarfs. These are the people of whom the Rav says that their growth takes place "solely within the public domain." A spiritual parasite is a man who has "never sought to render an accounting either of himself or of the world; never has he examined himself, his relationship to God and his fellow men. He lives unnoticed and dies unmourned. Like a fleeting cloud, a shadow, he passes through life and is gone. He bequeaths nothing to future generations, but dies without leaving a trace of having lived. Empty-handed he goes to the grave, bereft of mitzvah performances, good deeds, and meritorious acts, for while living he lacked any sense of historical responsibility and was totally wanting in any ethical passion. He was born involuntarily, and it is for this reason, and this reason alone, that he involuntarily lives out his life (a life which, paradoxically, he has 'chosen'!) until he dies involuntarily. This is man as the random example of the biological species" ("The Halakhic Man").

This, it goes without saying, is also the man who is totally unaware of his ontological needs. Not that he is aware of such needs and dismisses them, but he is in a state in which needs can be understood by him only in sensual, economic, or social terms. And since most people interpret needs in quantifiable, visible, assessible terms, man, in the life order we live in, ejects himself into the visible outside and truly believes that this is the truth of existence.

SELF-DECEPTION AS A LEGITIMATE WAY OF LIFE

Most people go about legitimizing self-deception with utmost sincerity. Jean-Paul Sartre, a master in describing the social and societal lie as a lived truth, describes self-deception as "a legitimate way of life." Self-deception, because it has become so prevalent and so unsuspicious, has thus become, for most people, a way of life. It has become, moreover, as Sartre puts it (in *Existentialism*), "something akin to faith. . . . It cannot be either a cynical lie or a certainty—if certainty is the intuitive possession of the object. But if we take belief as meaning the adherence of being to its object, when the object is not given or given indistinctly, then self-deception is a belief. Let us understand clearly," Sartre goes on, "that there is no question of a reflective, voluntary decision, but of a spontaneous determination of our being. One puts oneself in self-deception as one goes to sleep, and one is *in* self-deception as one dreams. Once this mode of being has been realized, it is as difficult to get out of it as to wake oneself up. Self-deception is a type of being in the world like walking or dreaming, an order which by itself tends to perpetuate itself."

The Rav sees this malaise the way Sartre does, namely, as a state into which man slips unconsciously. Let us repeat the Rav's words on the subject: "He is neither conscious of his assignment vis-à-vis something which is outside of himself, nor is he aware of the existential otherness as a being summoned by his Maker to rise to tragic greatness." There are, then, two kinds of lies man tells himself: one is the moral lie, that is to say, the lie he has to live within the fated dichotomy of his existence as a dialectical being, and there is the immoral truth of natural man embracing the dreadfully artificial, yet seemingly natural social principle as if there were no other principle in the world to live by.

TO FIND REDEMPTION IN SURRENDER

Nothing, probably, would strike natural man as so inconceivable as the idea that there can be anything redemptive in surrender, even in surrender to a higher moral will of which he knows nothing at all. "Natural man," the Rav writes, "unaware of the element of tension prevailing between the human being and the environment of which he is an integral part, has no need to live a normative life and to find redemption in surrender to a higher moral will" ("Confrontation").

"To find redemption in surrender to a higher will" is the essence of *teshuvah*, which is, above all, the establishment of a personal relationship with that supernal moral Authority. *Personal* is the key word. And not just personal, but intimately personal. The Rav, in one of his typical distinctions between the natural man, who is a "something in general," and a someone in particular, speaks of "cosmic man" who finds God (if ready for Him) in the vastness and boundlessness of the cosmic drama, in heavenly galaxies billions of light years away. By contradistinction, and here we come back to the grandeur of the *tzimtzum*, origin-minded man, as the Rav puts it, "finds God in the limitedness and narrowness of finitude, in the smallness of the modest home into which man was born and to which he willingly returns. He discovers God in the origin, in the source, in the center of the burning bush. Either infinity cannot contain God or God, if He so wills it, addresses man from the dimensionlessness of a point. What is the center of a bush if not a point? And out of that point God spoke to Moses" ("Catharsis").

Contrary to natural man, who can think of God—if he does think of Him—only in terms of impersonal, cosmic expansion, there comes Halakhic Man, who detects God in the point of His "contraction," His *tzimtzum*.

HE WAS RIGHT THERE

Of course, in moments of joy and elation, one finds God's footsteps in the majesty and grandeur of the cosmos, in its vastness and stupendous dynamics. In such moments, moments of ecstasy, God, as the Rav puts it, addresses Himself to man through the twinkling stars and the roar of the endlessly distant heavens. In such moments, *majestas Dei*, which not even the vast universe is large enough to accommodate, addresses itself to man and fills him with creative joy.

The Rav, however, also at home with "the dark night of the soul," speaks unhesitatingly of "moments of agony and black despair, when living becomes ugly and absurd, plainly nauseating"; of times when man loses his sense of beauty and majesty, and stands bereft of hope. In such moments, says the Rav, God addresses man not from infinity, but from the infinitesimal; not from the vast stretches of the universe, but from a single spot in the darkness which surrounds suffering man, from within the black despair itself.

The Rav resorts here to a tragic personal experience: the loss of his wife. When his wife lay on her deathbed, with no hope for recovery, he watched her dying, day-by-day, hour-by-hour. Medically, he could do very little for her. In fact, nothing. All he could do was to pray. However, the Rav writes, he could not pray in the hospital. Somehow, he could not find God in the whitewashed, long corridors, among the interns and the nurses. However, the need for prayer was great; he could not live "without gratifying this need." The moment he returned home, he would rush to his room, collapse on the floor and pray fervently. "God in those moments appeared not as the exalted, majestic King, but rather as a humble, close friend, brother, father. In such moments of black despair He was not far from me. He was right there in the dark room. I felt His warm hand, as it were, on my shoulder. I hugged His knees, as it were. . . . He was with me in the narrow confines of a small room, taking up no place at all. God's abiding in a fenced-in, finite locus manifests His humility and love for man. In such moments, *humilitas Dei*, which resides in the humblest and tiniest of places, addresses itself to man" ("Majesty and Humility").

I doubt whether any of the great confessions penned by the masters of world literature contains anything that can be compared to the sacred simplicity of a soul so humbled by painful love as that which comes spontaneously to the fore in the Rav's confession. What the Rav describes in this shattering personal account of sorrow is equally heartrending and thought-provoking. To have an irresistible need to pray when there is still a glimmer of hope is one thing. But to have this need—and one must never lose sight of the Rav's accent on inner needs—when all hope is gone, is awesome. How can this need for prayerful communion overwhelm one who is in a state of total hopelessness? How can it be understood, moreover, that the need, at such moments, can express itself in feelings so extraordinarily tender?

One cannot help but feel that the Rav must have experienced, in that tragic state, the truth and the mystery of Divine descent—that is to say, of His *tzimtzum*, or contraction, as understood by the Lurianic Kabbalah. In those moments, the Rav says, and we repeat, "He was not far from me; He was right there in the dark room. . . . I felt, as it were, His warm hand on my shoulder. He was with me in the narrow confines of a small room. . . . In such moments, *humilitas Dei*, which resides in the humblest and tiniest of places, addresses itself to man."

MAJESTAS DEI AND HUMILITAS DEI

And what does man, so addressed, do in such moments? We do not know what the Rav said in his prayers, but one may venture to assume what he didn't say. He did not say, "*Eli, Eli, lamah azavtani?*"—"My God, my God, why hast Thou forsaken me?" For, no, he *did not* feel forsaken! He may have felt wounded, grieved, sorrowful, crushed, but no, not forsaken. How can one feel forsaken with God's "warm hand on his shoulder"? How can one permit this closeness to God to be undermined by the remoteness of His help? The unanswerability of these questions deepens the dialectical mystery. "Man meets God not only in moments of joy and triumph, but also in times of disaster and despair, when God confronts him in the narrow straits of finitude: "*mima'amakim*"—"*min hametzar*"—out of the straits. Then he encounters not *majestas Dei*, but *humilitas Dei*, God's glory compressed into the straits of the human finite destiny. It is self-evident that the humility experience has to express itself in another set of ethical value judgments, in a unique morality. We do have two moralities, one of victory and triumph, one of withdrawal and defeat" ("Majesty and Humility").

To the Rav, as mentioned, the morality of withdrawal and retreat is rooted precisely in the ancient and ever-living mystery of the Divine *tzimtzum*, the Divine contraction, as explicated, but by no means confined to, the Lurianic Kabbalah. The Infinite God (metaphorically speaking) "retreated" in order to make room for a finite world. "He created the world by engaging in a movement of recoil."

DEFEAT IS BUILT INTO THE VERY STRUCTURE OF VICTORY

The Rav asks: "Is the Lurianic doctrine of *tzimtzum* just a kabbalistic mystery without any moral relevance for us? Or is it the very foundation of our morality? If God withdrew, and creation is a result of His withdrawal, then, guided by the principle of *imitatio Dei*, we are called upon to do the same. Jewish ethics then requires man in certain situations to withdraw" ("Majesty and Humility").

Man must not always be victor, says the Rav. From time to time, triumph should turn into defeat. Man, in Judaism, was created for both victory and defeat—he is both king and saint. He must know how to fight for victory and also how to suffer defeat." Modern man is frustrated and perplexed because he cannot take defeat. He is simply incapable of retreating humbly. Modern man bombasts quite often that he has never lost a war. He forgets that defeat is built into the very structure of victory, that there is, in fact, no total victory; man is finite, so is his victory. Whatever is finite is imperfect; so is man's triumph" ("Majesty and Humility").

THE SOCIAL DIMENSION OF THE PRINCIPLE OF WITHDRAWAL

"Guided by the principle of *imitatio Dei*, we are called upon to do the same. Jewish ethics then requires man in certain situations to withdraw."

How can the principle of withdrawal be applied to the socioeconomic realm? The Rav, who defined Adam the first, that is to say, the nonconfronted, aggressive, victory-obsessed man, as one whose motto is "success, triumph over cosmic forces" ("The Lonely Man of Faith"), saw him, as it seems obvious, as a man incapable of *retreat*. It is, in the Rav's words, "the cosmos [which] provokes Adam the first to quest for power and control." With the cosmos in mind, Adam the first is bound to think in terms of *expansion*, that is to say, to quest not for what is true but for what is functional, pleasant, and dominant—for things, in other words, which are rooted, at best, in the aesthetic, but by no means the noetic-ethical sphere. "Adam the first," the Rav writes (in "The Lonely Man of Faith"), wants to reclaim himself from a closed-in, nonreflective existence by setting himself up as a dignified, majestic being capable of ruling his environment." The adjectives "dignified" and "majestic" here signify social status or economic and political power. We are dealing here, in other words, with success as expansion but by no means as growth. And expansive man is very far from knowing what is meant by "a redeemed existence."

By contradistinction, man who aspires to the experience of a redeemed existence must accept the dialectical thought of retreat and recoil as the gateway to a sacred little corner where the Infinite God can be experienced in "the narrow straits of finitude." In order to get to that "point" he must, by the same token, accept the other dialectical paradigm that "precisely because of the supremacy of the intellect in human life . . . the Torah requires at times the suspension of the authority of the logos. . . . The Judaic concept of *ḥok* represents human surrender and human defeat. . . . In a word, withdrawal is required in all areas of human endeavor; whatever is most significant, whatever attracts man the most, must [at times] be given up."

There are some well-intentioned Jews who earnestly ask some very pointed questions. "We are looking to experience God," they say, "and you give us the *Shulḥan Arukh*, a compilation of laws telling us how and when to daven, what to eat, and how to conduct our married lives. Why should we bog down in minutiae when we are searching for the Infinite?" (Rabbi Harold S. Schulweis, *In God's Mirror*).

The Rav's answer should be obvious by now: Judaism abhors

bottom lines! The only bottom line known to Judaism is the one that Hillel gave to a non-Jew who aspired to embrace Judaism, and it was of a purely ethical nature, for in Judaism the ethical and the meta-ethical are bound together. The Judaism that is molded in the *beth medrash*, however, that is to say, in *lernen*, is fully aware that bottom lines dealing with laws of how to daven, what to eat, and how to conduct our married lives are meaningless to a person who wants to "experience God" without having first experienced the Torah.

Here we have another case where retreat and recoil is needed for the sake of an ultimate advance: retreat and recoil from the generality of a religious abstraction to the particularity of halakhic minutiae, the ardent and extended study of which is the only way leading up to the "experience" of God. Franz Rosenzweig was making precisely this point when he said (in *The Star of Redemption*) that the revealed law itself is the primary source for our knowledge of revelation. We must stand within revelation, he writes in truth, to know it. "Prior to the soul's acknowledgement of Him, He cannot let Himself be recognized by it." This clarifies what the Rav means by the "finitization of the Infinite" as the gateway to the infinitization of the finite. What some liberal Jews like to refer to as "narrow-mindedness" is quite often the *min hametzar*—the "straits," the narrow straits, the psalmist is talking about. The straits may be those of sorrow and distress, but they can also be of restriction and obedience. Out of the straits, the vast areas of the *merhavyah* may well be in sight. The answer to the call out of the straits is heard, as the psalmist tells us, "in the vast areas": finitization invites the answer of the Infinite.

OBJECTIVE AND SUBJECTIVE TRUTH

It is, of course, very difficult to subject oneself to the minutiae of the law, for, contrary to the embracing of the Infinite, which is, as the Rav puts it, "subjective religiosity," obedience is the acceptance of the a priori "objectivity" of the Halakhah. Kierkegaard regarded subjectivity as a condition for the religious experience. "Truth is subjectivity," he insisted. But there is no contradiction here. The Rav identifies objectivity with the revealed law, while to

Kierkegaard subjectivity meant inwardness. The Rav would have no objection to this, for it is out of the subjection to the a prioristic objectivity of the revealed law that the singular human personality emerges in all its splendorous subjectivity and uniqueness, as the Rav characterizes the halakhic man. Here we are dealing with a man who is the opposite of a "something in general," as Kierkegaard defined the immediate man. Here we have the somebody in particular par excellence!

THE CURSE OF THE SOCIAL IMAGE

We asked before how the principle of withdrawal can be applied to other areas of human life which demand revision. Let me just mention one of them, typical of so many in the outward-oriented life order of which Sylvia La Shawn, the American author, speaks in her book *The Crisis of Middle Age*. It deals with a published interview with a well-known American couple, true "celebrities," who happened to be her friends, and who seemed to prefer the social image over the redemptive truth.

"What a perfect, totally untroubled life was described in that interview! Such a sharing, such happiness, such a richness and completeness of living, such joy! The model marriage, the perfect family, the beautiful people living the gorgeous life. . . . I know these people. I know their problems, their courageous struggle to overcome difficulties, to grow, to become more real to each other, to find their own selves in a deeper, more meaningful way. The truth about them is far more beautiful than the perfect story, the perfect happiness described in the interview. The truth is so full of such poignant humanity that I felt sorry for the thousands of readers who devour such stories and really believe it is possible to be so perfectly happy. By now we know that the books and films we grow up on don't tell the truth about life, that they are lying to us."

And they are lying to us because we want to be lied to, because we ourselves lie to ourselves out of fear of facing ourselves as we are. The masses need to be lied to because it provides them with an escape from a dreary reality. But how is one to understand the lying of those "beautiful people" whose story, the true story, not the public facade was, in fact, so humanly meaningful not in spite of, but precisely on account of, its tragic nature?

The answer lies in one word—"tragic." The aesthete—and it was aestheticism with which, seemingly, that couple were stricken—as an Adam-the-first type, in the Rav's definition, regards tragedy with suspicion. His motto being "nothing succeeds like success," he is in most cases incapable of grasping that there are cases in life when "nothing *fails* like success." What we mean by this has been illustrated of late, for example, by the sad stories of the Wall Street insiders who were driven to ruin, to jail, and to despair just because they did not know of the existential, let alone the moral and even economic necessity of making the movement of recoil and retreat before it was too late. The diabolic power that stood in the way of such a retreat was greed. When people know not the secret of recoil and retreat, greed is on the ascent.

The couple which Miss La Shawn told us about fitted perfectly the Rav's and Kierkegaard's description of the aesthete. Since the aesthete is dignity-minded, and since dignity to him means primarily the way he is seen by others, he is deeply involved in the world of immediacy. The aesthete, Kierkegaard says, is essentially a driven man, even if he thinks he is pursuing a life of purpose. He is easily fascinated, but just as easily tires of everything. Solely concerned with himself, he is unable really to communicate. Kierkegaard maintains, and the Rav would not disagree with him (since to him sin is an aesthetic sin), that the aesthetic mode knows its form of suffering too, but it is caused by the environment, not by a genuine inner struggle.

This Kierkegaardian thought (in *Either/Or*) that the aesthete knows his mode of suffering, too, but it is caused by the environment rather than by any genuine inner struggle, may define the story of La Shawn's couple, so typical of many other celebrities. Inner suffering caused by the environment, not by an inner struggle, is common among those who are unaware of the redemptive power of recoil and retreat precisely in face of an ununderstanding social environment. The only environment which will understand it is the one which knows understanding as a mode of being in the world. It is not in vain that the Rav mentions, on more than one occasion, that the deepest friendship imaginable is among talmidei ḥakhamim.

ONTOLOGICAL AND SOCIOLOGICAL NEEDS

The Rav stresses the fact that Maimonides incorporated in the Halakhah dealing with the fundamentals of prophecy, i.e., that God causes man to prophesy, a description of the personality and spiritual stature of the prophet. "And with good reason," the Rav says, "for the image of the prophet and the structure of his consciousness are also parts of the principle of prophecy; they serve both as man's telos and as the ideal of ethical perfection, as posited by Halakhah—i.e., that man should know that among the species of man there are to be found men whose nature is such that they possess exalted and refined moral habits and great perfection, and their souls are ready until they finally receive the form of the intellect. Afterwards the human (acquired) intellect will cleave to the active intellect, and there will overflow from the active intellect to the human intellect a mighty overflow. These are the prophets and this is prophecy" ("The Halakhic Man").

That is the state of a person who has fulfilled his task as creator. But even the aspiration to acquire such a state, an aspiration inherent in the soul of the Torah scholar, is enough to ennoble and refine him to a point of true authenticity. Such souls are in search of each other, in need of each other, and in love with each other. Such souls, in fact, spiritually feed on each other. They know their needs as they know to distinguish between ontological and "sociological" needs which they are sometimes called upon to renounce.

When the Rav says, as he does, that man is "doomed" never to find out what his real needs are, we can only attribute this pessimistic view to the despair that often seizes the best among us at the sight of man's growing ignorance of his true needs. In order to be able to do so, man must recreate himself.

That is why, when it comes to the vital notion of self-recreation, the Rav is much less pessimistic about man's ability to know his real needs. We thus read: "By activating his intellect" (and by "intellect" the Rav means the *ratzon elyon*, the higher will of which the Torah is the ultimate expression) "man finds himself on the road of discovering ultimate redemption. When man recognizes himself, he dissipates not only ignorance, but also the mist of anonymity. He is not unknown anymore: he knows himself and finds freedom in this knowledge. *He is aware of his needs* because he prays. He is aware of his intellectual creative capacities because he *studies*. He is sure that the needs are his own and that his intellectual capacities are part of himself. This twofold knowledge is cathartic and redemptive'' ("Redemption, Prayer, Talmud Torah").

IN ALL THY WAYS KNOW HIM

The Rav himself provides the definitive answer to the existential question whether man can ever acquire a true need-awareness. Commenting on the biblical passage "In all thy ways know Him, and He will straighten out your paths" (Prov. 3:6), a passage which the sages characterize as "a small portion on which hangs the whole matter of Torah" (Ber. 53a), the Rav says, "To believe is necessary, but it is not enough: one must also feel and sense (in all his ways) the existence of God. The Presence of the Almighty must be a personal, intimate experience. And if this experience is not common, and if it proves impossible to achieve that *devekut* (cleaving) to Him, blessed be He, and if one feels not the touch of His hand, one cannot be a complete Jew" ("On Repentance").

To explain it better: when there is the great awareness of knowing Him "in all thy ways", He will make you aware of the paths of your other needs. He will "straighten them out" for you. In other words: Deed-awareness will bring about a state of need-awareness.

Does the Rav promise peace of mind in return for need-awareness? No, not peace of mind. One gets the impression, moreover, as one studies the Rav, that the very thought of peace of mind appears to him as something akin to camomile tea, good for the simple-minded or the cult-ridden neophyte. What the Rav *does* promise is a wider self—"a wider self," as William James put it, "through whom comes a saving experience."

The Rav calls this "a redemptive experience" and applies it to *teshuvah*. Never losing sight of the great moments of joy and inner freedom which the *talmid hakham* experiences in his pursuit of Torah knowledge, the Rav regards the religious act as "essentially one of suffering. When man and God meet, man is called upon by the Divine to embark upon a course of self-sacrifice which is manifested in a struggle against his primitive instincts, in a breaking of the individual will, in the acceptance of a 'transcendental burden,' in an occasional dissociation from the pleasant and attractive, and in an addiction to the bitter and strange.' 'Make sacrifices!'; that is the command governing the religious man" ("On the Love of the Torah and the Redemption of the Soul").

This "make sacrifices" requires an explanation, and it is provided, strange as it may sound, by Miss La Shawn's aforementioned celebrities. Had they known the creative and, indeed redemptive meaning of "making sacrifices," they would have known (1) that suffering must never be treated as a social embarrassment, as most people do; and (2) that retreat and recoil from the success syndrome must never be regarded as failure. Had people in a happiness-oriented society known the true meaning of making meaningful sacrifices, they would have spared themselves the awful sense of futility that goes together with making sacrifices in vain. The need to make the right sacrifices is man's real need-awareness.

"The beauty of religion, with its grandiose vistas, reveals itself to man not in solutions, but in problems, not in harmony, but in the constant conflict of diversified forces and trends" ("*Kodesh* and *Hol* in World Perspectives").

The religious experience, even on a very high level, does not lead man here below to paradise, but to paradox, the Rav says. That was, and remains, after all, the paradox and the promise of Jacob "wrestling with God and prevailing"—prevailing, yes: but with a wound in his body.

That is the fate of what the Rav refers to as the "covenantal faith community": it rises to the tragic and heroic heights of a "community of destiny" by means of the wound—the undying symbol of its eternal wrestling with God and with man, and prevailing.

5

Sin-Sickness and *Teshuvah*

METAPHYSICAL CORRUPTION AS SICKNESS OF THE SPIRIT

When the Rav speaks of sin as a metaphysical corruption, he is speaking of a malaise which afflicts the spirit, or *ru'ah*. Between the *nefesh*, which is the animal, or vegetative, soul in man, and the *neshamah*, which is the emanation of the Supreme Intelligence and constitutes man's resemblance to the Divine, there is the *ru'ah*. The sicknesses which afflict the *nefesh* are of a distinctly clinical nature. Those which afflict the *ru'ah* are defined by the Rav as metaphysical corruptions. Since it is the spirit which imbues existence with meaning, sickness of the spirit, or metaphysical corruption, may condemn existence to oscillate between vacuity and anxiety.

Does this mean that the pure of soul are immune to sickness of the spirit? Not all all. The pure of soul and sound of mind, in fact, may very well be familiar with pain, sickness, and suffering, but, first, they will not permit it to bring them down, and second, they will treat it as a means of purification and refinement. Thus suffering may provide them with an opportunity for the leap into the heroic on which the Rav places so much emphasis precisely because it is so closely related to the tragic!

The Rav sees suffering the way the psalmist sees it—dialectically. Thus, when the psalmist says, "Troubles have enlarged my heart" (Ps. 25:17)[1]—for that is exactly what it says!—he touches upon the heart and the secret of creative suffering: *tzarot*, "trou-

---

1. Wrongly translated as "The troubles of my heart have increased."

ble," is closely related to *tzar*, "narrow." There is a tendency in most suffering people to fetishize themselves, so to speak, on their suffering as if there were nothing else in the world. They narrow themselves down to a state of brooding exclusively on their *tzarah*. For the psalmist to say, as he does, that "*tzarot* have enlarged my heart" means that they, the *tzarot*, have imbued his suffering with meaning, or, more exactly, that he actually grows on pains that would make most people shrink. The sicknesses of the sinner, however, are rooted in this narrowness of heart. Since sinners are not sensitive enough to detect the malaise of defilement in themselves, they are also incapable of regarding their sicknesses as clarion calls for purification—the highest form of repentance.

Maimonides devotes a large part of his *Eight Chapters* (Commentary on Avot) to repentance, and the Rav often refers to the "Great Eagle," particularly when it comes to the symptomatology of sin. Some of the symptoms seem very familiar to ears attuned to present-day mental problems. The process of repentance, as seen by Maimonides, is by no means a "quick fix" or an easy "seeing of the light," but a continuous effort of the heart and mind which may last for many years. It originates in a sense of guilt, or remorse, of a feeling of lostness, of spiritual bankruptcy, of worthlessness, of frustration and failure, all of which are, according to the Rav, symptoms of sin-sickness in its various forms and manifestations. The recovery in such an acute case of inner vacuity is long and difficult, and repentance takes place only when the penitent, helped by the Torah he embraces with an embrace of cognitive love, undergoes a complete metamorphosis. Complete metamorphosis thus implies not just the possibility, but the definitive realizability of the new law of causation.

MENTAL SICKNESSES AND SPIRITUAL SICKNESSES

The recovery from sin-sickness is, in other words, a lifelong process. Sin-sickness being a metaphysical corruption, requires a much greater therapeutical effort than "mental sickness." The Rav observes in his master thesis "On Repentance" that the term "sickness of the mind," as used by Maimonides, Rabbenu Baḥaya, and other medieval sages, does not refer to mental sickness such as insanity, but rather "to a moral deficiency, that is to say, to sin, which informs man that he is ill. If sin is an illness, then it, too, must be felt, i.e., must be expressed in and through suffering. Every organic illness or abnormality reaches the awareness of the human being through his nervous system. The language of illness, its A-B-C, is suffering. . . . The organism informs the human being by means of suffering that he is ill. Suffering, according to Aristotle, is a great blessing conferred by the Creator on His creatures; it serves as a warning of what to expect. Indeed, we all know how many tragedies are liable to occur because pain is discovered when it is too late" ("on Repentance").

The Rav asks: "We all know, to our great sorrow, what bodily pain is. In what way are spiritual suffering and the suffering of sin expressed? How is man made aware of the sickness of sin?"

The Rav, in reply, speaks of sin as an anti-aesthetic experience.

SIN AS AN ANTI–AESTHETIC EXPERIENCE

This, it seems to this author, is an astonishingly new and relevant approach to the question of what constitutes sin. We never thought of sin as an aesthetic aberration, did we? A violation of some ethical laws—yes, of course. An affront to religious principles—definitely. But how can we see it as an anti-aesthetic experience?

Soren Kierkegaard defines three stages of human development: the aesthetic (which could easily accommodate hedonism), the ethical, and the religious. The Rav, however, himself armed with all the dialectical weapons of existential thought, sees it differently. To him, the aesthetic, in the final account, cannot be divorced from the ethical, and if it tries to assert itself independently of the ethical norm, it should disqualify itself as an arbiter even on what, as an example, constitutes art. Nor can it be otherwise. For the aesthetic mode of living, as Kierkegaard saw it, shows man as deeply involved in the world of immediacy. "The aesthete," Kierkegaard writes (in *Either-Or*), lives in the moment and tries to forget all continuity and personal involvement in his life." The aesthete is essentially a driven man, even if he thinks he is pursuing a life of purpose. He is easily fascinated by outward appearances, but just as easily tires of everything. And in this pursuit of the senses and the sensual, which in the final account is an endless chasing after enjoyment, or, as we call it today, "fun," man is really unable to communicate on a level of dialogue because, no matter what he says, he is solely concerned with himself.

Even here, in Kierkegaard's thoroughly negative portrayal of the aesthete, symptoms can be detected of an effort he must make to free himself—in spite of his alleged independence from the ethical demand—from his own conscience. If the aesthete, as Kierkegaard puts it, lives in the moment and tries to forget all continuity and personal involvement in his life, he is, spiritually speaking, depersonalized. But can this depersonalization ever really succeed? Since Kierkegaard extends his treatment of the aesthete to include the hedonist, or "intellectual aesthete," that is to say, the contemplative who tries to stand, as it were, outside life and behold it as "a spectacle," it is clear that to Kierkegaard, the aesthetic attitude could be only partial. It cannot possibly cover the WHOLE man. The aesthete himself, particularly in his intellectual disguise, may seem to be satisfied with his role, but only partially so. He is committing the unpardonable sin of the thinker's speculative detachment from life.

The Rav, in line with the neo-Kantian notion of the "moral law within," goes further than Kierkegaard when he declares, in his inimitable fashion, that "an Abigail follows every sinner." The allusion is to the biblical Abigail. We read (in 1 Sam. 25:36–37): "And Abigail came to Nabal and, behold, he held a feast in his house, like the feast of a king; and Nabal's heart was merry within him, for he was very drunken; wherefore she told him nothing less or more until the morning light. And it came to pass in the morning, when the wine was gone out of Nabal, that his wife told him these things, and his heart died within him, and he became as a stone."

What did Nabal do? Soulless, lawless potentate that he was, he tried to handle his neighbor's possessions as if they were his own. That neighbor happened to be David, and the possessions happened to consist of his flocks. Upon hearing about Nabal's criminal deed, David marched against him with four hundred of his men. Abigail, whom the Bible describes as a woman "of good understanding and of a beautiful countenance," came up to David, not yet king, and pleaded for mercy. She told him exactly what she thought of her husband: "Nabal is his name, and folly is with him.'' She pleaded, however, with the God-anointed to spare her husband's life, not because he deserved it, but to prevent bloodshed in Israel. David thanked and blessed her. If not for her sake, he told the righteous woman, there would not have been left to Nabal ''any that pisseth against the wall.''

The Rav interprets Nabal's reaction to the news of the threat to his life in the following manner: ''This has been the way of sin since the beginning of time. It overtakes man while indulging in a night of iniquity. Mist and fog conceal the inner light of the soul of a man who is immersed in the blinding, obsessive night of his passions and is plunged within the oblivion of his lust. At the very hour when 'Nabal's heart was merry within him' he was in such a state of intoxication that he did not notice the flashing blade of the sword hanging over his very door.'' Abigail did not break the news of his doomed state to her husband right away. She waited ''until the morning light'' when the ''wine was gone out of Nabal'' and informed him that his fate now lay in David's hands. She knew when to speak and when to hold back. As the Rav puts it, ''There is a time when moral criticism is effective and a time when any discussion with the inebriate sinner is impossible, and nothing anyone says can penetrate his hearing or enter his heart.'' It takes time, but in the right time, it comes to pass. ''And it came to pass in the morning when the wine was gone out of Nabal . . .''

AN ABIGAIL WATCHES OVER EVERY SINNER

''Rest assured,'' the Rav exclaims, ''an Abigail watches over every sinner.'' Abigail saw her husband in his revelry, that is to say, in his flagrantly hedonistic behavior. This is quite often the state of the aesthete as the hedonist, or ''immediate man,'' in Kierkegaard's terminology. All that Nabal experienced when he realized that David was on his heels was momentary shock. He was, after all, an arch-case of the depraved man. Not only did his name testify to it (*nabal* = ''lawless''), but even his father's name, Belial (''without an above,'' i.e., ''godless''). Nabal was just shaken, speechless. However, the Rav emphasizes, most people are capable of anticipating the arrival of an Abigail. There is such a thing, in the Rav's view, as a sense of remorse which strikes man almost as soon as he sobers up from the drinking party. He suddenly, or slowly, grasps the implications of his sin. They are: failure, despair and spiritual bankruptcy. "To sin" (*hata*) actually means "to miss" (*le-ḥahti*) the target. The sinner, at bottom, is a misser!

THE SECOND GREAT SIN AFTER CAIN'S

Little do we ponder, hardly even realize, the astonishing fact that the first anti-aesthetic sin in the Bible was only second, in its far-reaching, devastating consequences, after Cain's sin of fratricide. It was a sin, an aesthetic sin, to be sure, which was not only indistinguishable from the ethical, but was the root-cause for the forming of hereditary character traits which are distinguishable to this very day. We are referring to another case of drunkenness. This time, however, not of an evil man, but of a good man: Noah.

The Bible tells us very precisely about the reactions of Noah's three sons—Shem, Ham, and Yaphet—to their father's nakedness. Ham notices it first and lewdly tells his brothers to come inside and look. His brothers, however, do something else. They take a blanket, and "walking backward" they throw it over their father's nakedness. The Bible does not tell us how Noah, upon awakening, knew what had happened; and it is here that the prophetic stance makes its first appearance.

First Noah blesses Yaphet—Yaphet, whose son, as Scripture tells us right there, is Yavan, the Hebrew name for Greece to this day. The blessing deals here, astonishingly and appropriately enough, with beauty: *Yaphet Elokim leyaphet*—"May God beautify Yaphet" (or "May God give beauty to Yaphet," or "enlarge it" in most translations). And that is exactly how Hellenism is defined to this day!

Next Noah blesses Shem with his "tent." The text says right there that Shem's son is Eber (i.e., "Hebrew"), implying the beauty of the spirit, contrary to Yavan's spirit of beauty, which the tent, a symbol of teaching, stands for in the Bible.

But when it comes to Ham, Noah curses. He does not curse Ham, however, but his offspring, Canaan. How is this to be understood? If we accept Abarbanel's opinion that certain biblical curses must be understood as prophecies, then Noah's curse is indeed verifyingly and terrifyingly prophetic. Samson Raphael Hirsch is very specific about the realization of this prophecy. For we must bear in mind that we are dealing here, as is obvious from the names of Ham's other children, mentioned in the same portion of the Bible, with some vast segments of Africa whose inhabitants were for many generations the victims of slavery or victimizers of slaves, and, in some areas, still are.

Was Ham's transgression of an aesthetic or an ethical nature? It was, as seems obvious from the story, *both*, for, as Scripture sees it, the aesthetic, unless "censured" by the ethical, degenerates into sheer vulgarity, and vulgarity is something that brooks no forgiveness. Little attention has been paid to this extraordinary narrative which establishes forever the severity of the law regarding vulgarity. We are dealing here with an internal truth which our contemporary hedonists, speaking of art as independent from ethical considerations, refuse to comprehend. Art, as an expression of truth or the search thereof, is not the laying bare of things, but, quite often, their discrete veiling. It was, after all, God Himself who, as the Bible tells us, made clothes for the first couple when they realized they were naked. Did He really have to make them Himself? He did, because that, too, was an act of creation, or creativity. The purpose of art is to refine life or, as Ortega y Gasset puts it, to console it. But refinement is unimaginable without a fusion of the aesthetic with, at least, the subliminally ethical.

AND THE PEOPLE MOURNED

To further illustrate his vital point that sin is an anti-aesthetic experience, the Rav (in "On Repentance") resorts to various biblical examples. The Torah, recounting the sin of the Golden Calf, tells us that "when the people heard these evil things, they mourned, and no man put on his ornaments" (Exod. 33:4). How can mourning be a reaction to sin? The Rav replies that in the wake of sin there comes a strong feeling of sorrow. The previous day, the people engaged in wild, joyous celebrations around the Golden Calf, but now they experience the bitter sorrow of mourning. Nor is this the only time that a sense of sin is expressed in terms of mourning. We come across the same phenomenon in the case of the spies: "And Moses spoke these words [of Divine reprimand] to all the children of Israel; and the people mourned greatly" (Num. 14:39).

How does the Rav explain this phenomenon? "According to Halakhah, the laws of mourning apply when a person loses something important and precious. The loss of money and property is not a real loss. A real loss is the loss of a dear and beloved person. Mourning is the reaction to a loss, and it expresses itself in a strong sensation of nostalgia, of yearning, or of retrospective memories. The power of mourning, its cruelty and its loneliness, has its focal point in the memory of the human being. . . . Memories float up from the past, and when the past comes to the surface and man is forced to compare yesterday to today, he is engulfed by a feeling of bereavement and mourning."

The sinner also mourns. What does he mourn? "He mourns that which he has irretrievably lost. What has he lost? Everything! The sinner has lost his purity, his holiness, his spiritual wealth, his joy of life; the spirit of sanctity in man; all that gives meaning to life and content to human existence." In brief, "the sinner mourns his own soul which he has lost" ("On Repentance").

The Rav's definition of the sinner as a man mourning his own soul which he has lost, and the association of sin-sickness with mourning over the loss, struck me as particularly relevant as I was reading through some case-histories of grave depressions described by famous patients. I will just mention one of them, William Styron, the well-known American author. In a terrifying little book appropriately titled *Darkness Visible*, he masterfully and unhesitatingly describes his own encounters with inner darkness. Speaking of the help he sought all over the professional circuit he writes, "Certainly one psychological element has been established beyond any reasonable doubt: and that is the concept of loss. Loss in all its manifestations is the touchstone of depression—in the progress of the disease and, most likely, in its origin." Mr. Styron goes on to say that "the loss of self-esteem is a celebrated symptom, and my own sense of self has all but disappeared along with my self-reliance. This loss can quickly degenerate into dependence [on drugs?] and from dependence into infantile dread. One dreads the loss of all things, all people close and dear. There is acute fear of abandonment."

Reading these lines by the noted author of *Sophie's Choice*, among other works, one cannot help but bring to mind that incomparable passage in the Psalms which affirms a condition that is the very opposite of lostness, namely the holding onto: "If Thy law were not my joy I would have been lost in my misery." Here the Torah emerges as a source of joy—a lost sensation in a pleasure-seeking world—and hence, contrary to darkness, visible, as a light invisible but experienced. "Light is sown for the righteous and joy for the pure of heart" (Ps. 97:11). Here one walks a path which is illuminated for him without his knowing that the light in front of him is projected by his own rightness.

SIN AS EXISTENTIAL DEFEAT

At the risk of repeating ourselves, we should mention again that commenting on the enigmatic passage in the Psalms, "And I said in my haste, every man lieth," the Rav asks: "What kind of lie did the psalmist have in mind when he hurled this serious accusation at man in general? Did he have in mind the lie which the 'I' tells the 'Thou'? Did he refer to the everyday social lie? Did he refer to the commercial lie of the dishonest businessman? to the political lie of the faithless ruler? to the judicial lie of the perjurer? In a word: did he speak of the profitable, immoral lie? Does man indeed engage constantly in immoral lying? By no means," the Rav answers. "The psalmist is concerned with a different kind of lie: the existential lie that man tells not others, but himself. Man is indeed a liar because he is involved in an unresolvable contradiction, in an insoluble dialectic. Because he is caught, like Abraham's ram, in a thicket of antinomies and dichotomies. He swings like a pendulum between two poles: the thesis and the antithesis, the affirmation and the negation, identifying himself either with both or with neither. He must lie, but this inevitable lie is rooted in man's uniqueness and is a 'moral' lie! It is the wellspring of human creativity. . . . That agony accompanies the process of human creativity is due to the fact that it is torn man who is the creator."

Here the Rav clearly reaches the summit of existential frustration, the kind of frustration that one encounters only very rarely, if at all, in authentic Hebrew thought, and which one hesitates to gloss over precisely on account of its originality and daring. Here the Rav actually states most emphatically that there is, as it were, a lie which is rooted in being, and is indispensable—as indispensable as his tornness. And it is not only that man really cannot do much about it, but that he should not go too far in fighting it. Without being immoral in any way, man's vital tornness—because it is a tornness which breeds creativity—is a necessary moral lie. Tornness, in other words, is true, it is a fact, but it is not *a truth*. One must distinguish between what is true and what is a truth. It is true, for example, that man is a wolf to other men, but it is not a truth; it is a truth that you are your brother's keeper, but it is not true. Tornness is factually and ineradicably true, but it is not a truth, not an eternal truth, and because it is not a truth, it is a moral lie, but an indispensable one. If it is torn man who is the creator, as the Rav maintains, then even the consciousness of being torn does not really absolve man from the moral lie he is doomed to live, almost as Sartre's existential archtype is, in his famous words, "doomed to be free."

But it is one thing to live a moral lie without being immoral, and quite another to live an existential lie—a real, "honest-to-goodness" lie—without being at all conscious of its *being* a lie. The Rav's bold commentary on the psalmist's "And I said in my haste, every man lieth" invites a juxtaposition of the conscious moral lie with the unconscious state of the aforementioned immoral truth. What comes to mind, in this context, is Tolstoy's classic story "The Death of Ivan Illich"—by now an existentialist text-book story. It provides a good example of what we mean by an immoral truth. Ivan Illich is a thoroughly ordinary, self-satisfied bourgois who lives his unperturbed, uneventful life in conformity with society. He has acquired, in the average way, a degree of success, has found love and marriage and a family in the average way, etc. One day, this rather likable, pleasant, sociable, and seemingly satisfied fellow falls from a ladder in his house, but the accident seems slight and he does not pay much attention to the pain in his side. As the pain persists, however, he begins to go from doctor to doctor, but no diagnosis seems to help. Then, suddenly, the horrifying thought dawns upon the middle-aged man that he is going to die. The reality of death does not lie in the physical structure of the organs that medical men keep on examining: it is the reality *within* Ivan Illich's existence. "To Ivan Illich," Tolstoy writes, "only one question was important: was his case serious or not? But the doctors ignored his inappropriate questions. From the doctors' point of view it was not under consideration: the real question was to decide between a floating kidney, a chronic catarrh, or appendicitis. It was not a question of Ivan Illich's life or death, but one between a floating kidney and appendicitis."

The reality of death, when Ivan Illich learns the truth about his condition, sunders him, initially at least, from all other human beings, including his own family. It thrusts him into a state of absolute solitude and obliterates in his mind the whole fabric of society and family in which he has lost himself all his life. As the end draws closer, he somehow begins to see through the unconscious artificiality and almost natural pretentiousness of his life. It now seems to him to be meaningless and devoid of any value he can hold on to to the bitter end. But as awful and inexorable as the presence of death is, it gives to the dying man the only revelation of truth in his life, even if the content of the revelation is the realization of the pointlessness of the way he has lived!

Was this a religious revelation or an existential hindsight? The Rav answers this question not in relation to the Tolstoy story, which he mentions on another occasion, but, as aforementioned, in his explanation of a crucial passage in the Psalms: "And I said in my haste, every man lieth." In the Rav's comment to that seemingly enigmatic passage in the Psalms, he emphasizes that it is the existential lie which the psalmist is talking about—a lie which can sometimes even be a moral lie. There seems to be little doubt that Ivan Illich, who recognizes only at the end of the road that he has lived a lie, never really regards it, maybe not even at the end, as an immoral lie. He has lived the normal life that is lived in society and in conformity with the rest. He must have had some easy "self-evident truths" which he shared with the others around him who, like him, took short views and in whose social gaze he had seen himself as they had seen themselves in his. He is not a liar. Very far from it. But he has lived, existentially speaking, a lie.

Tolstoy does not tell us anything about the role of religion in the life of Ivan Illich. We must assume, however, that he is, like everybody else, a church member; but that in the face of death, church membership, too, is devoid of meaning for him. What Tolstoy tried to do in his classic story is to prove that death does not have to validate the truth of God, for it is enough if it invalidates the lie of a life lived, in the psalmist's word, *lashav*, "in vain." At the end, it seems that Ivan Illich is mourning more the life he never really lived than the death he is going to die.

The Rav's example of the people "mourning" after the sin of the Golden Calf is thus exact: the children of Israel found themselves mourning their misdeed as one mourns an irretrievable loss. They stood mournfully face-to-face with the God of life, as the hero of the Tolstoy story stands face-to-face with the truth of death, which reveals to him that his life was a lie, a self-deception.

AMNON AND TAMAR

The biblical story of Amnon and Tamar is well known, and the Rav resorts to it as to a starkly vivid example of another facet of sin-sickness: self-disgust. "The feeling generated by sin," the Rav writes (in "On Repentance"), "is not a moral sensation. The moral sense in man is not such a powerful force. The feeling of sin which drives a person to repentance is an aesthetic sensation or, more exactly, a negative aesthetic sensation. The sinner feels disgust at the defilement of sin. The suffering of sin lies in the nausea toward the defiling, disgusting uncleanliness of sin."

To illustrate this point, the Rav quotes from II Samuel 13: "And it came to pass after this that Avshalom the son of David had a fair sister whose name was Tamar; and Amnon the son of David loved her. . . . And Amnon was so vexed that he fell sick for his sister Tamar, for she was a virgin, and Amnon thought it hard for him to do anything to her." In his vexation, he feigned sickness and sent a royal messenger to summon Tamar to prepare for him, so was the excuse, some food. When she came, he pleaded with her to lie with him. She vehemently, and pleadingly, refused, but to no avail: he raped her. It is obvious, of course, that Tamar, to whose beauty Scripture testifies, had seemed to Amnon irresistible to the point of sickness: he took sick out of love for her. No other love, by the way, is so drastically described in the Bible. Her pleadings with him not to do "this base deed" and not to behave "as one of the base men" did not help. He forced her to yield to his passions, after which a sudden, violent metamorphosis overtook the sinner. "And Amnon hated her with a great hatred; for the hatred with which he hated her was greater than the love with which he had loved her. And Amnon said unto her, 'Arise, begone!' " (v. 15). Dreadful, isn't it? And not only dreadful, but inexplicable. So sudden? So cruel? Could this be the same Amnon who took sick—sick!—out of love for her?

The Rav explains: "He hated her now with such a great vengeance not because he suffered pangs of conscience, but because he suddenly realized not only that she was not beautiful, but how ugly and repulsive she was." How come? Because we are dealing here with the abominable. "His sin was an abomination to him. . . . Because of it he came to hate himself—and, consequently, hated her. Sin has a masochistic effect. Amnon hated himself and transferred his hatred to Tamar. Humiliated through no fault of her own, the same wondrously beautiful Tamar was transformed in his mind into a symbol of abomination and hate. Amnon certainly did not understand what had happened to him, and he asked himself the same question which the author of the *Hayei Adam* asked: 'We are astonished—I am astonished at myself: How could this abomination have been committed?' "

Earlier in his seminal work "On Repentance" the Rav has something to say about the *Hayei Adam* and its author, Rabbi Abraham Danzig.[2] "It is interesting to note," the Rav writes, "how an elderly Jew in the old-fashioned city of Vilna—the author of the book *Hayei Adam*—many years ago understood so well the aesthetic opposition a person builds up towards sin. The natural inclination or desire of man is for the beautiful, for the aesthetic.

---

2. Mention should be made here, in passing, that Rabbi Abraham Danzig is better known by the name of his book than by his own name. This is also the case with various other *talmidei hakhamim* who were the authors of books of lasting importance, some of whom did not even mind their real names remaining unknown; among their number are the Hafetz Hayim, in his earlier years, and the Hazon Ish in our own generation. This uniquely Jewish tribute to some of the great sages—and by sages we mean pillars of Halakhah who remained known by the names of their books—bears testimony to the Rav's contention that it was not the synagogue, but the bet medrash, the house of study, which played the dominant role in Jewish life.

Man despises the ugly—it is this which draws him away from the sin into which he has sunk, inasmuch as sin contains ugliness, disgust, and abomination, which repel man's aesthetic consciousness. Thus when God seeks to draw man to repentance, He arouses not only his moral awareness, which is usually not sufficiently strong to awaken him from his sin, but, more so, his aesthetic consciousness, which has better chances of affecting the despised and loathsome sin. The sinner begins to ask himself, in the words of the author of the *Ḥayei Adam* (in his *Tefilah Zaka*), 'We are astonished at ourselves: How was this abomination perpetuated?' "

ARISE, BEGONE!

"Arise, begone!"

Tamar's pleas not to "add this greater wrong of sending me away to the other that you have done to me" are in vain. Amnon calls in his servant and orders him "to put this woman out of here." Even Tamar's name now seems abhorrent to him, for he refers to her as "this woman." As we read the story, we are astonished not only at Amnon's abominable deed but at the abominable manner of his reaction to his abominable act. Are we dealing here with a form of reactive sin-pathology which surpasses the horror of sin-pathology itself?

While we wholly accept the Rav's explanation of the transformation which suddenly occurred in Amnon's turbulent soul, we find it difficult to accept the thought that "these were," in the Rav's words, "the natural reactions of revulsion and shame, and not processes of reason, understanding, and knowledge." We have no problem with the second part of the explanation, but by what stretch of the imagination can we accept the idea that Amnon's reaction was "the natural reaction," etc.? Of course, Amnon's abominable deed in sending away his raped sister, the king's daughter, in shame and humiliation, was due to his identifying her, as the Rav puts it, "with the sin itself," but is it not possible that there was more to it than identifying her with the sin itself? Wasn't there here an unconscious attempt to loudly and wildly call for his own punishment? If sin, as the Rav says, is born with its own punishment, doesn't the Amnon story come to confirm it?

It appears from the biblical account of the outrage that Amnon did all he possibly, and pathologically, could to assure that his crime would be made public. When he ordered his male servant to throw Tamar out, he knew, of course, that the woman he had ordered thrown out into the street—where, by the way, she put ashes on her head as if she were in mourning—was the king's daughter. In no time, all of Jerusalem must have known of Amnon's crime. And that, in turn, was enough to seal his doom. Avshalom, his own outraged brother, killed him.

That sin ultimately avenges itself on the sinner is a biblical axiom, as it is written: "Evil shall slay the wicked" (Ps. 34:22). What this means is not only that sin is the cause of punishment from without, but that it quite often serves as the cause of self-punishment—and even of unconscious self-punishment—from within the afflicted psyche. If the afflicted psyche is aware of the reason for its affliction, it may lead to repentance; if not, to self-destruction.

A modern-day example would not be out of place. According to reliable statistics, the percentage of suicides among homosexuals is three times as high as among heterosexuals. The protestations and demonstrations of "gay pride" are nothing but pathologically spurious attempts to overcome the sense of self-disgust and abhorrence which most homosexuals, no matter what they say, experience about themselves.

SIN AND NEUROSIS

Sin, as mentioned, is seen by the Rav as something which is not only displeasing to God, but sickening to man. Thus, there is a close connection, as Kierkegaard saw it, between sin and neurosis. Since the sickness that sin causes is not, and should not be perceived as, "a form of punishment, or a fine, and is not really imposed in the spirit of anger"—for it is a "metaphysical corruption of the human personality," as the Rav puts it—we are led to the awe-inspiring and, indeed, soul-restoring realization that repentance is an act not only of placating the Creator, but of restoring the self as His partner in creation. Sin, in other words, is de-creation. Repentance is the creation of a restored self. If "the acme of moral and religious perfection, which Judaism aspires to, is 'man the creator,' " the Rav writes (in "The Halakhic Man"), "the Almighty, when He created the world, left room for his creature-man to participate in His creation. It was as if the Creator 'spoiled' reality so that mortals might set it right and modify it. God transmitted the mystery of creation—the Book of Creation—to man not only that he might read it, but in order that he might carry on the act of creation. God left an area of evil and chaos in the world so that man might make it good. The abyss breeds misfortune and trouble, and chaos lies in ambush in the dark alleys of reality, desiring to undermine the Absolute Being and subvert the radiance of creation."

CATHARSIS, TESHUVAH, AND SIN-SICKNESS

"God left an area of evil and chaos in the world so that man might make it good." How does man face the area of chaos and evil in the world with any hope whatsoever to contribute toward its diminution?

The Rav's answer would be that one can face this area in the general, intellectual, and scientific domain by means of catharsis, and in the Judaic domain by means of *teshuvah*.

Teshuvah is Catharsis, but catharsis is not necessarily *teshuvah*. *Teshuvah*, moreover—and we mean *teshuvah* as the antidote to metaphysical pollution—is cognitive and cumulative. Catharsis is a spontaneous response to man's ontological needs—the need for purpose and meaning in life. *Teshuvah* is the fulfillment of the need itself.

The Rav thus advances the thought (in "Catharsis") that Judaism insists upon catharsis as a redemptive gesture in all areas of human endeavor, including the intellectual. Judaism, in other words, maintains that there is an "unredeemed cognitive gesture," just as there is "an unredeemed carnal drive." The Rav explains that by such a "gesture" he does not refer to mythical thinking, which is not guided by scientific method and precision, but to the most modern methods of scientific inquiry. In what way can the latter be considered "unredeemed"? It is unredeemed, says the Rav, if the scientist does not subject his cognitive act to "an extraneous catharsis" which consists in the dialectical movement, that is to say, marching forward, inspired by victory, and retreating one step in defeat. By this, the Rav further explains, he does not mean to suggest that the scientist should conduct his inquiry without thoroughness, or inconclusively. "On the contrary, every scholar is guided intuitively by an ethical norm which tells him to search the truth assiduously and not to rest until he has it within his reach. Cognitive withdrawal is (thus) related not to scientific inquiry as a logical operation, but rather to the axiological experience of scientific work." In other words, "knowing" is not an impersonal performance which can be emptied of its rich, colorful, experiential content. "It is an integral part of the knower as a living person. Next to the religious experience, knowledge is perhaps the most vibrant and resonant personal experience. It sweeps the whole personality of the knower, sometimes like a gentle wave, at other times like a mightily crushing tide. This is a form of catharsis—the catharsis of knowledge—which takes place not in the formal, logical realm, but within the *experiential*. Commitment to knowledge, to scientific inquiry, implies ipso facto the recognition of the eternal mystery which grows with the advance of knowledge."

"If the scholar," the Rav goes on, "simultaneously with the ecstasy of knowing, experiences also the agony of confusion, and together with the sweetness of triumph over being, feels the pain and despair of defeat *by* being, then his cognitive gesture is purged and redeemed. Then and only then does his gesture become heroic" ("Catharsis").

What the Rav is stressing, in his notion of catharsis as the ideal state in which knowledge "sweeps the whole personality of the knower," is an existential maxim which Kierkegaard expressed in his own way, with Nietzsche following in his footsteps. What Kierkegaard rose against is precisely the separation of the knower from his knowledge. To him "the philosopher of systems" can be compared to a man who builds a castle, but lives next door in a shanty, or the other way around. Such a fantastical being does not himself live within what he thinks; but the thought of a man must be the house in which he lives or it will become perverted.

Catharsis, therefore, as perceived by the Rav, is unthinkable without intellectual honesty, if not humility. Since it involves not only advance, but acceptance of defeat, the ethical norm outweighs the power of the ego and thus assumes a heroic dimension.

To engage in the redemptive act of catharsis, particularly in the case of cathartic *teshuvah*, is possible only if and when retreat is measured by halakhic standards. That is to say, retreat as a condition for growth—be it in the religious or the intellectual area. This movement of retreat, or so to say, withdrawal, paradigmatic to Halakhah, involves withdrawal from certain freedoms which are, existentially speaking, vacuums. The inability to withdraw may seem at first to increase one's ability to advance, but it sooner or later turns out to be an advance in a void. It is this void which is the breeding ground of sin and, ultimately, of sin-sickness.

Does this mean that halakhic man is free from all these symptoms? Here we come to one of the truly baffling aspects of the Rav's dialectical thought, the one in which he himself becomes, as it were, "dialectical." We have, on the other hand, the Rav's bold assertion that when the halakhic man "approaches the world, he is armed with his weapons, i.e., his laws, and the consciousness of lawfulness and order which is implanted within him serves to ward off the fear that springs from him." We hear him assert that "such concepts as nothingness and naught, chaos and void, darkness and the abyss, are wholly foreign to him. His entire world is 'builded with turrets' (Song of Songs 4:4); layer upon layer, and he, the halakhic man, may be compared to the guard which surrounds the palace of the king, 'where the watch is only for the sake of His glory' (Maimonides, Laws of Sanctuary 8:1)" ("The Halakhic Man").

How do we reconcile this happy mood about the therapeutic power of Halakhah with a personal statement which bespeaks an entirely different state of mind? "Let me speak for myself: I know that I am perplexed, that my fears are irrational, incoherent. At times I am given over to panic; I am afraid of death. At other times I am horrified of becoming, God forbid, incapacitated during my lifetime. One of my greatest fears is related to the observance of the Day of Atonement; I am fearful that I might be compelled, because of weakness or sickness, to desecrate this holiest of all days."

DESPAIR AT SELF-INSUFFICIENCY

"I don't know what to fear, what not to fear; I am utterly confused and ignorant. Modern man is indeed a slave, because he is ignorant and fails to identify his own needs" ("Redemption, Prayer, Talmud Torah").

In these last words we discern the deeper reason of the Rav's inner dichotomy: it is a despair at his self-insufficiency. The great man, in his humility, demands so much of himself that he is not satisfied with what he has already achieved. After all, "He is rich who is satisfied with his lot" was not said of the soul! So the Rav, it seems, is at times "in despair," to use a famous Kierkegaardian line, "at not being himself," or, more exactly, at not being enough of himself. But that is not all. To this author it seems that the two sides of the Rav—the halakhically optimistic and the ontologically pessimistic—would have been on a collision course only if it were to "assign," so to speak, to the *yetzer hara*, the so-called sinful urge, an exclusively negative role in human nature, something the sages of the Talmud were careful not to do. Without it, they knew, the creative urge, rooted in free will, would not have been possible. The Rav's insistence on the vital role of polarity in human nature, as the source of man's creativity, thus implies not only the need for the *yetzer*, but—and this has not been appreciated enough— the acquired ability to differentiate between the *yetzer* as an evil urge and the *yetzer* as the source of a vital existential restlessness, even if bordering at times on despair. Albert Camus was right when he said that "there is no consolation in this world for a man of real compassion." It follows that real compassion, rendered even more real by human helplessness, may very well be the justified—religiously justified—cause for fear, confusion, and indeed, darkness at noon.

The Rav interprets the familiar passage in Esther, "for one cannot come to the gate of the king's court dressed in rags," to suggest that one cannot serve God in "the rags of despondency." For a man familiar with despondency to make such a statement is equally tragic and heroic, particularly since, like Mordechai of old, he too, is constantly aware that there are so many Hamans in the world, Alas!

AND SO FEW MORDECHAIS

Yes, and so few Mordechais. Abraham the "Hebrew" and Mordechai the "Jew" (*Yehudi*) represent for all the generations that have followed them the essence of Judaism: eternal warfare against idolatry. "And Mordechai does not bend and does not kneel" epitomizes the raison d'être of Judaism to this very day. But what do we mean by idolatry when we speak about it in actual, contemporary terms? The Rav distinguishes between idolatry and paganism—very much alike, but by no means identical. There is a form of idolatry in the world which has almost destroyed it and which expresses itself in the fact that millions of people accorded to a Hitler, a Stalin, a Mao Tse Tung, a Sadam Hussein the treatment reserved for deities. But this treatment, lest we forget, has been accorded not only to mighty tyrants but to charismatic, nontyrannical rulers—in fact, to so-called liberal rulers in whom people have had absolute faith.

"We may trust man," the Rav writes, "have confidence in him, but we may not have *faith* in him. Faith connotes absoluteness, and no man is worthy of absolute faith. Faith is solely applicable to God." The Rav goes on to say that the incisive validity of this judgment was demonstrated during the war years when the President of the United States, Roosevelt, refused to bomb the railroad systems leading to the crematoria and concentration camps.

"American Jewish leaders," he writes (in "The Profundity of Jewish Folk Wisdom"), accepted the transparent rationalization of the State Department that intervention would have hampered the war effort. Why did American Jews not act like Mordechai, who, when he heard the evil decree, "went into the center of the city and shouted bitterly and loudly" (Esther 4:1)? Why were there no public demonstrations with mass tearing of garments, as Mordechai did, to awaken Jewish leaders and to arouse the conscience of Christian America? Had we responded like Mordechai, would President Roosevelt have acted as callously as he did? . . . Apparently what inhibited Jewish action was the faith that American Jews had in the President: their adulation bordered on idolatry. But for this idolatry, millions of Jews would probably have been saved. President Roosevelt was a great leader for America, but he was a disaster for the Jews. If he had been President in 1948, Israel would probably not have come into being, so mesmerized were we by our faith in him. The *Hashgahah* chose Harry Truman to be the instrument of God's purpose. We had trust and confidence in Truman, but we never exalted our regard for him.''

IDOLATRY AND PAGANISM

Speaking of the difference between the *egel hazahav* (Golden Calf) and the *Kivrot Hata'avah* ("Graves of Lust"), the Rav explains that idolatry, as practiced in antiquity and as manifested by the *egel hazahav*, signified actual worship, ritual and cultic perform- ances. It involved specific acts to propitiate deities presumed to reside within the idols. Paganism, by contrast, is not a mode of worship but "a cultural system, a manner of living." Paganism, in other words, is idolatry stripped of supernaturalism. It is the *yetzer* as sheer seduction. Our sages were convinced, says the Rav, that idol worship inevitably and ultimately leads to paganism. "Yet paganism can persist even after idol worship has been discarded. The later Greeks and Romans, having cast aside idol worship, still lived as pagans, with a pagan life-style and value system. In our day, with idol worship no longer in existence, paganism is still rampant" ("The Profundity of Jewish Folk Wisdom").

Paganism, in the Rav's definition, appears as a malignant out- growth of the Adam-the-first type of man. The pagan worships deities which represent forces of nature, but since they are without moral norms they make no demands of man beyond specific acts of propitiation, without a trace of even the daemonic. For man lustily to partake of nature is to see himself, as the Rav puts it, as "coextensive to nature" and thus "to crave unlimited indul- gence." To worship nature is, in this context, nothing but the worship of one's *own* nature, which, unsubmitted to the code of do's and don'ts, is to regard anything possible as permissible. "The antithesis to paganism," the Rav writes, "is expressed in the verse 'And follow not the desires of your heart and your eyes which lead you astray' " (Num. 15:39).

The hedonist, however, who identifies libertinism with free- dom, is, in actuality, a slave to a form of paganism which is worse than idolatry. For idolatry, in its cultic, supernatural sense, can, with little effort at persuasion, be proven wrong. For paganism, however, to be proven wrong, one must do away not only with superstition, but with the diabolical habit, so typical of the life order, of looking outside for oneself, that is to say, of existential ignorance. This ignorance is the sinister power that lurks behind the pagan's attitude to freedom. Just one example should suffice: it is easy to become an enthusiastic follower of an organization like the American Civil Liberties Union. But it takes much more than stale liberalism—so rampant today, alas!—to understand that the freedoms it protects may degenerate from civil to uncivil liberty, from the outcry against human injustice to the defense of inhuman justice. That is why the fundamental dualism, as Nicholas Berdyaev puts it, "is not the dualism of natural and supernatural, nor the dualism of material and psychical, nor the dualism of nature and civilization, but the dualism of nature and freedom, nature and spirit, nature and personality" (*Slavery and Freedom*).

This is a thought, a vital thought, which is lost in the life order where paganism reigns supreme. The Rav rightly remarks that the Torah detested the pagan way of life more than it hated idol worship. The Kivrot Hata'avah (What a name!) revealed that even without idol worship paganism still exercised its hold upon the people, a vestigial remnant of their long stay in Egypt." The Torah describes the *ta'avah*, the lust, with which the Israelites in Kivrot Hata'avah gathered and devoured the quails, and we see before us a people in the mire of a gluttonous orgy, a rite of wild insatiability. "And the people rose up all that day and all that night and all the next day, and they gathered the quails; he that gathered least, gathered ten heaps, and they spread them out all around the camps" (Num. 11:32).

"The text," the Rav comments, "speaks only of the unlimited gathering of quails. The sages, however, tell us that this was a rebellion against all inhibitions. It expressed itself in a repudiation of the sexual code just recently prescribed on Mount Sinai. . . . The oral tradition, as expressed by the sages, understood Kivrot Hata'avah as an orgy of the senses, an idealization of unrestricted indulgence." Prior to that explosion of *ta'avah*, a paganistic sin which Moses found even more revolting than the idolatrous sin of the Golden Calf, the Israelites were warned to master their cravings and discipline their indulgence, but to no avail. The Rav writes: "Kivrot Hata'avah" was not idol worship, but paganism. The latter is *peritzut*, unlimited lust, sexual wantonness, boundless desire, and sensual indulgence—the hypnotic and the orgiastic, what the Greeks meant by *hedone*. One can argue and persuade effectively against idol worship; but what does one do with paganism, which is morally nihilistic? It is not a competitive and alternative discipline; it is not a discipline at all. How does one teach the superiority of a restrictive but ennobling system which wants man to identify with God and not to be a child of nature?" ("Teaching with Clarity and Empathy").

This is the question which our generation, if it is to save itself from a pagan liberalism, masquerading as freedom, will have to confront before it is too late.

6

Sin as Spiritual Pathology

THE DIABOLICAL HABIT

The Rav, never given to exaggeration, uses the harshest possible adjective, "diabolical," to define the extreme state of confusion about himself in which man finds himself today: "the Diabolical habit of man to be mistaken about his own needs." The word "diabolical," which the Rav would not have used unless he felt that we are dealing here with dark and maddening forces at work, now more than ever, in and around the human psyche, requires elucidation. But before we go into it, a few clarifying words on the Rav's concept of *teshuvah*, or repentance, would be in order.

The most startling aspect of the Rav's concept of *teshuvah*, as expounded with extraordinary erudition in his seminal work "On Repentance," is its existential dimension.

Teshuvah, as it emerges from the Rav's treatment, is something one must do not only in order to restore oneself, as it were, to the good graces of God, but to regain one's own self-esteem. One does *teshuvah* not only to please his Maker, but to recreate oneself. With *teshuvah*—real *teshuvah*—a new self is born. If the message of Judaism, as the Rav puts it, is that "man was created to create himself," the need for self re-creation is particularly relevant today in view of the undeniable, indeed pitiable, impoverishment of the spirit which characterizes technological society. What follows this process of despiritualization is not only an intoxication with materiality, but an entanglement in confusion. Never before was man more confused about himself than today. That is what the Rav means when he speaks about "the diabolical habit of man to be mistaken about his own needs." Sin, according to the Rav, is the imp of this habitual perversity.

The sinner, in the Rav's thought, appears not only as a moral delinquent, but as an existential failure. Hosea 14:2, "Return, O Israel, unto the Lord, for you have failed in your iniquities," epitomizes the Rav's view of the sinner. This passage does not say, as it is usually translated, "for you have fallen," but "for you have *failed*." The Hebrew word *kashaltah* means "failed," not "fallen." The difference should be obvious: "You are not just sinners, but failures. Your sins have made spiritual cripples out of you. You have failed existentially, not just religiously."

If such a statement could have been made about sinners in any other period of history, it can be made with double emphasis about the period we live in. And this is not necessarily because our generation is more sinful, but because it is more lost: because it has lost its conception of sin. Otto Rank, who went much deeper than his former friend and mentor, Dr. Freud, in his understanding of the insufficiency of modern psychology to tackle the human predicament, spelled it out very succinctly in his definition of the neurotic: "The neurotic type suffers from a consciousness of sin as much as did his religious ancestors, without, however, believing in the conception of sin. This is precisely what makes him neurotic: he feels a sinner without the religious belief in sin, for which he therefore needs a new, rational explanation."

This state is truly "diabolical," as the Rav calls it. Man is rendered powerless to cope with his neurosis because of an acquired inability to accept the consciousness of sin—sin in the religious sense—as a condition for a redemptive catharsis. Ernest Becker rightly stresses (in his *Denial of Death*) that both Rank and Kierkegaard reached the same conclusion, namely, that "at the very furthest reaches of scientific description, psychology has to give way to 'theology'—that is, to a world-view that absorbs the individual's conflicts and guilt, and offers him the possibility of some kind of heroic apotheosis. Man cannot endure his own littleness unless he can translate it into meaningfulness on the largest possible level. Here Rank and Kierkegaard meet in one of those astonishing historical mergers of thought: that sin and neurosis are two ways of talking about the same thing."

That is exactly what the Rav is talking about, and that is also why he regards man's inability to recapture his lost conception of sin as a diabolical development. Without a conception of sin, man is reduced to a state of fetishizing himself on a fragment of reality and regarding it as the whole. Man is born a torn creature, the Rav says,[1] as is the whole of creation, which waits for its *tikkun*, or mending. Man's tornness, however, used to "evolve," so to speak, within a cosmic whole: because he measured himself against something that is larger than life, even what is "smaller" than life acquired a wider frame of reference. Now torn man dwells in a fragment of the whole and regards it as the whole of the whole.

This is truly a diabolical situation, for in such a state man loses any idea of his true needs and substitutes them with artificial definitions and rationalizations borrowed from a bankrupt, yet arrogant, reductionist world-view which insists upon the biological or behavioristic interpretation of man. Abraham Maslow calls this interpretation "cognitive pathology," and William Blake, who foresaw this diabolical development with the advent of the Enlightenment, spoke in horror of the rise, at some future date, of the "single vision" man. This man is here already, alas. It is this man who, on the one hand, "cannot endure his own littleness," as Becker puts it, but, on the other, cannot escape it either. His perception of sin is lost and, along with it, any idea of what his inner needs are all about.

It is truly a diabolical situation when man, unaware of his true inner needs, fetishizes himself on the very littleness which he cannot escape. The absolutization of the relative, which takes place in such a state, often even as a prescribed therapeutic method, thus turns into an existential menace. For when the relative is absolutized, it tends and pretends to provide final solutions to questions which man has been wrestling with since time began and whose grandeur lies precisely in the permanence of the wrestling! The spirit rejects final solutions, definitive answers, for spiritual liberation is conflict. The Rav stresses this point time and again. It is rooted not in common universals but in human specificity, which points, in its hoped-for emergence as

---

1. Rav Kook, like the Rav, spells this out unhesitatingly: "Whoever said about me that I am torn within was right. We cannot at all imagine a person who is not torn within. . . . Man's task is to reconcile the antinomies in his soul, but this is only an ideal we are striving for" (*Ma'ayan Divrei Viduy*).

personality, upward, not downward. The predominance of the social or societal principle can therefore be described as diabolical because it has so often made caricatures of vulgarity out of the very same people who make a fetish out of seeing themselves in each other's gaze.

This is particularly true of some aspects of psychoanalysis, which, no matter what its proponents say, induces the patient to fetishize himself on his littleness, i.e., childhood repressions. Those may be important, but by no means omnipotent. Rank saw this approach as destructive. Man, he says, in truth, wants to focus his love on an absolute measure of power and value. He wants to find and experience the marvelous, and the analyst tells him how matter-of-fact everything is, how clinically explicable are our deepest ontological motives and guilts. "Man," Ernest Becker comments, "is thus deprived of the absolute mystery he needs, and the only important thing that then remains is the man that explained it away, and so the patient clings to the analyst with all his might and dreads terminating the analysis" (*The Denial of Death*).

AT THIS JUNCTURE SIN IS BORN

If man has always been in a state of crisis—man, after all, *is* crisis—this crisis has been greatly aggravated by his scientific fragmentation, against which existential philosophy rose up in arms. A strange thing has happened to us on our way to the great new technological life order. We embraced a way of life which sees needs only in quantifiable terms. It is no longer important what a person *is*, but what he *has* or how he *appears*. Nicholas Berdyaev, the lucid Russian emigré philosopher, saw this state as one in which man "has ejected himself into the exterior," a state which, in his view, is bound to produce "second-rate human beings" (*Slavery and Freedom*").

Another existentialist philosopher, Karl Jaspers, speaks more specifically of the symptoms of this process of ejection into the exterior. Essential humanity, he says, is despiritualized and reduced to the general; to vitality as a functional corporeality. Joy is replaced by "fun." Public affairs become mostly entertainment; and private affairs, the alternation of stimulation and fatigue. There is a constant craving for novelty; not of meaningful, new thoughts, but the sensationalist novelty of the media and the disposable paperbacks whose inexhaustible current, quite often muddy and vulgar, flows swiftly into the waters of oblivion.

"There is no continuity," in Jaspers' words, "only pastime. Positivism (the malaise of our time) likewise encourages an unceasing activity of the impulses common to all, and enthusiasm for the numberless and the vast, for the expansive creations of modern technique; for huge crowds, and boundless admiration for the achievements, fortunes, and abilities of outstandingly (successful) individuals." What also follows is the willful complication and brutalization of the erotic; the bravura and machismo attached to the firing gun; the gambling, adventurousness, and even the hazarding of one's life, as of anybody else's life, which stands in the way of the acquisition of power. What man can do nowadays, Jaspers observes, can only be done by one who takes short views. He has occupation indeed, but his life has no continuity. "It seems as if the world must be given over to mediocrities, to persons without a destiny, without a rank or a difference, without genuinely human attributes" (*Man and Crisis*).

Could this have been said about any other generation? Other generations were, of course, less able to satisfy their needs, but they knew more than we do that there are needs which transcend the visible, the assessible, and the quantifiable in life. It is our generation—or the last two or three generations—that the Rav is talking about when he says that what contemporary man fails to comprehend is not the world around him, but the world within him, particularly his destiny and the inner needs of which he is supposed to have a clear awareness.

Man, the Rav says, is, of course, aware of many needs. In fact there are too many needs that claim his attention. An entire technology is bent on generating more and more needs in order to give man the opportunity to derive pleasure out of the gratification of artificially fabricated needs. This, however, the Rav avers, "does not contradict my previous statement that man is unaware of his needs. Man is surely aware of what he calls his needs, but the needs he is aware of are not always his own. At the very root of this failure to recognize one's truly worthwhile needs lies man's ability to misunderstand and misidentify himself, i.e., to lose himself. Quite often man loses himself by identifying himself with the wrong image. Because of this misidentification, man adopts the wrong table of needs which he feels he must gratify. Man responds quickly to the pressure of certain needs, not knowing whose needs he is out to gratify. At this juncture, sin is born. What is the cause of sin if not the diabolical habit of man to be mistaken about his own self?" ("On Repentance").

In other words, the needs, the real needs, are always there, hidden in the recesses of the soul, but man, in his ontological ignorance, renders himself incapable of identifying them. And since the real needs belong to the domain of the spirit, and the spirit is the most neglected, least understood, if not altogether suppressed of our potentialities, the suppressed ontological needs give rise to what the Rav refers to as "a spiritual pathology." We shall better understand the Rav's diagnosis of our fallenness as pathological if we resort for elucidation to some modern theories associated with existentialist psychotherapy, where sin appears as an existential sickness.

But before we do so, mention should be made of, and stress be put on, the Jewish notion of freedom of choice, a notion which the Rav, going in the footsteps of other sages of the Torah, stresses, emphasizing that freedom of will actually allows man to adopt a new law of causation. This is undoubtedly the most far-reaching, the most optimistic, and at the same time, most difficult task with which the Torah entrusts man. It entrusts him with the task of undoing causal predicaments, and it professes faith in his ability to do so.

Freudian determinism, which regards man as a prisoner of childhood repressions which he can at best identify but can hardly get rid of, may have some clinical validity, but it by no means has existential validity. Man's problems, as the Rav sees it, are due not only to childhood repressions, but to the suppression of spiritual growth in adulthood. That is to say, to "his diabolical habit to be mistaken about his own needs." Man's character, like his psyche, is by no means predetermined. If it were, freedom of choice would be a meaningless hypothesis. Characterological and psychological causes are subject to change, and if the change is of a revolutionary nature like *teshuvah—teshuvah* understood as self-re-creation—man can indeed make the heroic movement toward Him who waits for his return.

By the proper cognitive effort of mind and soul—and we stress, as the Rav does, the cognitive—man can liberate himself not only from undesirable habits but from undesirable traits, even from fear and anxiety. Man can free himself from what is bad in him by using what is good in the bad—the passionate energy of the *yetzer*—to energize the good. But there is one thing from which man, according to the Rav, can never free himself: the unseverable umbilical cord, as the Rav puts it, which, consciously or not, draws him to God. God, as it were, "inhabits the deeper recesses even of the sinner's soul, for "He dwelleth with them in the midst of their defilement" (Lev. 16:16).

The Rav explains this religious attraction, which is there whether man is aware of it or not, by concentrating on the deeper meaning of the High Holy Day Confessional, which starts with the words *Al ḥet sheḥatanu lefanekha*. This is usually translated to mean "For the sins we have sinned before Thee." The Rav, however, interprets *lefanekha* (from *panim*, "face") to mean "I have transgressed while standing before thee," that is to say, "in thy face."

IN THY FACE

For Judaism views man as standing before God—always. It does not accept a division between the two worlds, one in which man stands before God and the other in which man flees from Him. "There is no fleeing from Him." The Rav interprets the passage in the Psalms which says "Back and front You have restricted me, and You have laid Your hand upon me" (Ps. 139:5) to suggest the quintessential Torah precept which sees the dialectical relationship between freedom and restriction, on the one hand, and between Infinity and contraction, on the other. "Man is always standing before God, whether he be in the study hall, the office, the synagogue, or the bedroom. At all times, wherever he may be, man is standing before the Holy One, blessed be He" ("On Repentance").

"When man sins," the Rav continues, "he creates a distance

between himself and God. To sin means to remove oneself from the presence of the Master of the universe: I was standing before You, and sin came and estranged me from You, and I no longer feel that I am 'before You.' The whole essence of the concept of repentance is *longing*, yearning, pining to return again to be 'before You.' Longing develops only when one has lost something precious. 'From afar the Lord appeared unto me' (Jer. 31:3). Sin pushes man far away and stimulates his longing to return" ("On Repentance").

Man, in other words, has ontological needs that crave to be satisfied. This is not just a religious but an existential need, and when ignored, it expresses itself, among other things, as the philosopher N. Berdyaev pointed out, in *Anxiety*. "Anxiety," he states in truth, "points upward." It points, in other words, to a spiritual insufficiency, the result of unsatisfied or, worse, unrecognized ontological needs. Man is free to choose, but when his freedom is understood as the absence of a normative fence around his freedom, it degenerates into lawlessness and the overthrow of the yoke of the Kingdom of Heaven. Freedomistic-hedonistic man is then stricken by an inverted spiritual claustrophobia.

It is not in vain that Kierkegaard—that great man Kierkegaard!—defines anxiety as "the dizziness of freedom." A freedom which is understood as unrestrictedness may very well degenerate into the carrier of a "nausea" caused by an inability to stop galloping along the nihilistic road to a vacuous nowhere. This dizziness—caused, as mentioned, by the total absence of restricting and limiting road signs—can only be cured by the apprehension of a presence. The vast and vital use which the Rav makes of the paradigmatic notion of Kabbalistic *tzimtzum* clearly points toward such an experience. The Shekhinah means the presence of a presence. Shekhinah, literally translated, actually means "presence," as it is written, "They shall make Me a sanctuary and I shall be present [*veshakhanti*] in their midst."

The Rav speaks in his treatise on *teshuvah* about the distance which sin creates between God and man. He quotes Isaiah, who says that "your sins distance you from God" (Isa. 59:2). Here again, distance clearly stands for absence, a void, a vacuum. The very opposite of a presence.

THE PRESENCE AND THE VACUUM

This distance, which the Rav describes in his treatise on *teshuvah* as the void which sin creates between God and man may very well be the extreme opposite of what is meant by standing "in His presence always." If one is truly in His presence, the vacuum, which is, at bottom, the experience of an absence, is no longer a threat, but this is a very rare state today for the existential vacuum, of which there is a great deal of talk in existentialist literature, has now assumed the nature of a creeping terror which afflicts a growing number of people in technological society.

The vacuum, as mentioned, is, at bottom, the presence of an absence. To be sure, as the Rav stresses, God remains in man also after he sins, but He is so remote that the sinner does not feel His presence. We shall call this state the absence of a presence. Then there is a state in which the sinner begins to feel God's absence and is beset by an existential dread and fear. We shall refer to this state as one of the presence of an absence. The third and highest stage, that of the presence of a presence, is embodied in the character of "repentant man." He embodies the experience which begins with a vague feeling of sin and ends with the redemptive sensation of a wondrous proximity to God. As the Rav sees it, between these two stages stands man as a creator of worlds, as he shapes the greatest of His works—himself.

There are, in brief, such things as the absence of a presence, the presence of an absence, and the presence of a presence. Thus, when the Rav speaks of experiencing God as a presence, he addresses himself, by implication, not only to its extreme opposite, which is an absence, but to the fear and dread it produces and for which there is a term in modern psychiatry—anxiety. The experience of a presence as a stabilizing numinous guidance system has been stressed by another existential philosopher, Gabriel Marcel.

Dealing as we do with the existential thought of the Rav, we might as well look into areas where religious existentialists hold similar views and where they differ. Starting with where they differ, as religious existentialists, mention should be made that Gabriel Marcel, whom we intend to quote, was a Catholic existentialist philosopher whose influence in France was considerable. What first strikes us as significant is the difference between his notion of presence and that of the Rav. It characterizes the two diametrically opposed views of man as seen by Christianity and Judaism. Even the area where Marcel and the Rav share similar views, like man's ontological needs—a thought introduced into existential terminology by Marcel and to which the Rav would readily agree—does not narrow the gap between what the Hebraic and Christian world-views understand under the rubric of "presence."

ONTOLOGICAL NEEDS

According to Marcel, it is in the process of attempting to satisfy one's ontological needs that a sense of mystery comes into prominence. The ontological need, Marcel maintains, is a need for being. However, as all philosophers since Aristotle are aware of, being is something that cannot be adequately described, certainly not as a natural order, that is to say, an order of objects to be approached by dispassionate and rational analysis. Being, as Marcel sees it, constitutes a center of value, therefore it can only be approached and "understood" by a subject that is itself enmeshed and interacting with it in an order of appreciation, love, and fidelity. To satisfy an ontological need, Marcel maintains, is therefore to find an appropriate target of awareness in something that could be a presence, namely "a radiating source of concern and love which we can respond to in an appropriate way."

The prototype for this kind of experience, as Marcel sees it, can be found in the case of two individuals in love. For the lover to stand back, objectify, dissect, and understand love is no longer to be in love. It is to treat the beloved as an object at a distance. To be in love, however, to fully participate in the grand experience, and to undergo the presence of the beloved is to be in the presence of what Marcel calls a "mystery." When men treat one another as tools or objects, that is to say, when they regard the other person as an "it" instead of a "Thou," there is absence. In such a state "the spirit of man is not engaged." This is a Buberism to which we can all agree.

But some other of Marcel's premises are questioned by Milton Kunitz in *The Mystery of Existence*. Kunitz, an arch-secular scientist, asks why Marcel refers to the kind of experience he calls "presence" by the use of the term "mystery." Kunitz sees in this the hidden lines of a connection with the traditional Christian treatment of revelation in Jesus. "The clue we are seeking," Kunitz writes, "is to be found in the fact that Marcel, despite his coming to Catholicism late in life, has been adumbrating all along a religious point of view."

Marcel, we should add for greater clarification, makes a distinction between "problem" and "mystery." The dehumanization of man, as we witness it today in every area of human endeavor, arises, according to Marcel, from "the scientific and problem-solving attitude." Mystery, by contradistinction, answers man's ontological needs by exposing him to "the presence of a radiating source of involvement and love."

Comes the Halakhah, as expounded by the Rav, and introduces a revolutionary dialectical thought totally foreign to Christian theology: there is a "scientific and problem-solving attitude"—the attitude Marcel derides—which actually exudes, on a high level of cognition, the kind of mystery which the Rav refers to as the "appearance of a mysterious transcendence in the midst of our concrete world" ("The Halakhic Man"). The Rav goes further and states that "an individual does not become holy through mystical adhesion to the Absolute, nor through mysterious union with the Infinite, nor through a boundless, all-embracing ecstasy, but rather through his whole biological life, through his animal actions, and through actualizing the Halakhah in the practical world . . . It is the will of God that His Shekhinah, His Divine Presence, should contract and limit itself within the realm of empirical reality" ("The Halakhic Man").

To the halakhic man, in other words, "the scientific and problem-solving attitude," when applied to the Halakhah, is in itself a mysterious process. The Rav sees in it an aesthetic, an ethical, a religious, an intellectual, and—to crown it all—a teleological experience! There is even something in it, the Rav avers, which resembles the physicist and his concern with mathematical formulae, the laws of mechanics, the laws of electromagnetic phenomena, optics, etc. The halakhic man thus applies religious law and halakhic analysis to the most essential parts of human existence and cerebral endeavor. He shapes a metaphysical outlook by unifying scientific thought with the values and longings of Torah as an experiential blueprint for a creative human existence.

The preceding discussion clarifies why the Rav's profound treatise on the philosophy of Halakhah, "The Halakhic Mind," reads like an organically fused, dazzling analysis of Halakhah, science and philosophy pointing together in the single direction of Revealed Legislation. It could only have been written by a man whose sweep of intellect is wide enough to cover the whole area which the Gaon of Vilna must have had in mind when he said that "he who lacks one 'hand' in the sciences will lack twenty 'hands' in the understanding of the Torah." The Rav, it seems, lacks none. Like the ideal *talmid ḥakham*, "he joins together 'precept to precept, precept to precept, line to line, line to line, here a little, there a little' (Isa. 28:10; 13). From the midst of order and lawfulness, we hear a new song, the song of creature to the Creator. . . . Not only the qualitative world bursts forth in song, but so does the quantitative world" ("The Halakhic Man").

The mystery here is that the halakhic man, while involved in the problem-solving efforts that go into Torah study—efforts often similar to those of a scientist—cannot possibly emerge from it, as is the case with the scientist, as morally neutral! This is the mystery of the problem-solving attitude of the halakhic man. And not only that, but the mysterious connection between the study of the law for its own sake and the ethico-moral refinement that comes into prominence along with another mystery: the mystery, to which every *talmid ḥakham* bears witness: the Torah as a presence which precludes the possibility of an absence—for what is the existential vacuum if not an absence?!

"Halakhah, like nature," Professor Twersky writes in the spirit of the Rav, "abhors a vacuum." That is precisely what the Rav had in mind when he depicted the halakhic man as personifying the meaning of the prophetic words about the man who "joins together precept to precept, precept to precept, line to line, line to line, there a little, here a little."

AND THEN THERE IS A PRESENCE

Small wonder, therefore, that the Rav sees the absence as something which constitutes a spiritual pathology. Thus repentance is not only a religious precept, but a spiritual therapy. Sin and repentance are, as it were, born together, and are interlocked and bound together in a single dialectical whole. They both constitute stages on the way to self-recreation via self-confrontation.

There are, according to the Rav, two modes of forgiveness—atonement and purification. They cover two different kinds of sin: there is the sin that binds, for which atonement or pardon provides a counterweight, and there is the sin that defiles, for which purification is the only possible treatment. The sin that defiles is the metaphysical sin and it exists in the domain of the man-God relationship. As the Rav sees it—going in the footsteps of the psalmist, Maimonides, and Rav Kook—sin deforms and damages the innermost parts of man where dwells the Shekhinah, that is to say, the Presence. It is, therefore, our contention that the Rav's notion of absence has its equivalent in what existential psychiatry refers to as the existential vacuum.

THE EXISTENTIAL VACUUM AS SPIRITUAL PATHOLOGY

We know by now that psychiatry in general, and psychoanalysis in particular, have failed to live up to the grand promises of their proponents and even less so to the great expectations of their patients. A strange situation has developed in recent years. The growing feeling of helplessness among psychiatrists and the cries for help of the masses of suffering people operate in perverse contrast to the constant psychologizing of the media. "Amidst the 'answers' provided by publications ranging in sophistication from *Readers Digest* to *Psychology Today*," Dr. Jacob Needleman writes (in *Psychiatry and the Sacred*), "millions seem quite simply to have accepted that their lives have no great direction and ask only for help to get them through the night."

Ever since the last world war—an ineradicable horror which consigned to inglorious oblivion such nineteenth-century anthems to autonomous man as Swinburne's famous "glory to man in the highest/the maker and master of things"—voices are heard here and there which demand new approaches to our growing mental predicament. One such voice, and a very convincing one, is that of Dr. Viktor Frankl. An Auschwitz survivor who emerged as a major force in the international psychiatric community, he now occupies the same chair that was once Dr. Freud's at the University of Vienna. It was Dr. Frankl who first coined the term "existential vacuum."

The seminar on logotherapy at the Harvard summer school in 1961 heard Dr. Viktor Frankl, the founder of what is now referred to as existential psychotherapy, or logotherapy, expound some of his ideas about the state of psychiatry today. Nothing, we should add, of what the eminent psychotherapist said thirty years ago has been in the least eroded by the passing of time. To the contrary, time has, if anything, served as a verification-test of his theories.

"The psychiatrist today," Dr. Frankl said, "is confronted with a new type of patient, a new class of neurosis, a new sort of suffering, the most remarkable characteristic of which is the fact that it does not represent a disease in the proper sense of the term. This phenomenon has brought about a change in the function, or should I say mission, of present-day psychiatry. In such cases, the traditional techniques of treatment available to the psychiatrist prove themselves to be less and less applicable."

Dr. Frankl went on to say that he has called this phenomenon the "existential vacuum." What he meant thereby, he said, is the experience of a total lack, or loss, of an ultimate meaning to one's existence—a meaning, that is, which would make life worthwhile. The consequent void, the state of inner emptiness, is, according to Dr. Frankl, at present one of the major challenges to psychiatry. In the conceptual framework of logotherapeutic teaching, this phenomenon is also referred to as "existential frustration" or "the frustration of the will to a meaning."

By the latter concept, Dr. Frankl explains, logotherapy denotes what it regards as the most fundamental motivational force in man. Freudian psychoanalysis centers its motivational theory on the pleasure principle. (According to Freud, the reality principle is nothing but an extension of, and ultimately operates in the service of, the pleasure principle, or, as one might call it, "the will to pleasure.") Adlerian individual psychology focuses on what is generally called "the will to power." In contrast to both these theories, Dr. Frankl, in his formulation of logotherapy, considers man to be primarily motivated—or shall we say ultimately motivated—by "a search for meaning to his existence, by striving to fulfill this meaning and thereby to actualize as many value-poten-tialities as possible." In short, man is motivated by the will to a meaning.

The psychiatrist today, Dr. Frankl argues, therefore finds him-self quite often in an embarrassing situation. He is now confronted with human problems rather than with specific clinical symptoms. One of these human problems, Dr. Frankl asserts, is the attitude—the patient's or the therapist's—to suffering. Patients, Dr. Frankl asserts, never really despair because of any suffering in itself. Instead, their despair stems, in each instance, from doubt as to whether their suffering is meaningful. "Man is ready and willing to shoulder any suffering as soon and as long as he can see a meaning to it."[2]

It is by now, however, common knowledge that psychiatry, not to say psychoanalysis, is simply not meaning-oriented. One finds it hard to forget and, if one may say so, forgive Dr. Freud, at this vacuous stage of our culture, for having stated, in his famous letter to Countess Bonaparte, that he who seeks a purpose and meaning in life must be regarded as sick. By now we realize, as some keen observers of the psychiatric scene have remarked, that psychoa-nalysis may very well be the very sickness that it undertook to cure. Psychoanalysis, in other words, seems at times to regard the pearl as the sickness of the oyster.

It is therefore no accident that a growing number of people have by now given up on what psychiatry, not to say psychoanal-ysis, can deliver on any of its major promises. What is missing in the domain of psychiatry is seemingly a form of therapy which gets underneath affect dynamics, that is to say, in Dr. Frankl's words, "which sees beneath the psychic malaise of the neurotic his spiritual struggles. . . . What we are concerned with is psychother-apy in spiritual terms" (*The Doctor and the Soul*).

Just one word, before we proceed, about the importance which existential psychotherapy attaches to the attitude of patients to suffering. Dr. Frankl quotes his disciple, Edith Weiskopf Joelson, who states (in *Logotherapy and Existential Analysis*) that by

---

2. There is a prayer attributed to the saintly Rabbi Levi Yitzhak of Berditchev which runs as follows: "I am not asking you, my Lord, to disclose to me the meaning of my suffering. But do tell me, pray, one thing: that my suffering has a meaning!"

attributing to unavoidable suffering the status of a positive value, logotherapy "may help counteract certain unhealthy trends in the present-day culture of the United States where the incurable sufferer (or even the curable sufferer) is given very little opportunity to be proud of his suffering and to consider it ennobling rather than degrading." The burden of the unhappy person is increased, she writes "since he is not only unhappy, but ashamed of being unhappy."

To be unhappy is one thing, but to be ashamed of being unhappy is one of the typicalities of a life order which regards "the pursuit of happiness" almost as a constitutionally guaranteed right. It is as if one were supposed to be happy all the time, and if one is not, one is either a failure in his own eyes or scared stiff lest he be so regarded by others.

A NEW KIND OF PATIENT

Another eminent existential psychiatrist, Dr. Rollo May, speaks (in *Love and Will*) about "a new kind of patient" which he and his colleagues in the profession are increasingly confronted with. "It may be surprising when I say on the basis of my own clinical practice and that of my psychological and psychiatric colleagues that the chief problem of people in the middle decade of the 20th century is emptiness.

"While one might laugh at the meaningless boredom of people a decade or two ago, the emptiness has for many now moved from the state of boredom to a state of futility and despair which holds promises of danger.

"We deal here," Dr. May asserts, "with a feeling of boredom, futility and despair attributable to the sense of powerlessness people experience when it comes to doing anything effective about their lives or the world they live in."

THE SINNER AS A NONCONFRONTED MAN

This sense of powerlessness, it seems to us, is what really haunts the nonconfronted man. To the Rav it is simply unthinkable that a man who truly confronts himself and the world around him could go in any other direction but that leading to *teshuvah*. *Teshuvah* is not just confrontation, but redemptive confrontation. The Rav, as aforementioned, took the essentially pietistic notion of repentance and imbued it with an existential meaning of extraordinary relevance for our day and age.

At the outset of our inquiry, we quoted Matthew Arnold's lucid thoughts on the distinction between Hellenism and Judaism. "It is very well," he writes, "to talk of getting rid of one's ignorance, of seeing things in their reality, seeing them in their beauty. But how is this to be done," Arnold asks, "when there is something which thwarts and spoils all our efforts?

"This something," Arnold replies, "is sin."

It is nothing short of astonishing how this nineteenth-century Englishman of genius came to regard sin from the human angle in exactly the same manner as the leading contemporary halakhist, Rav Soloveitchik, regards it today from a purely Jewish angle: as something which is, as it were, *inimical to life.*

For the sin we are talking about, or, more exactly, the sin which the Rav is talking about, is, as mentioned before, something that we do not only against God, but against ourselves. Sin is not just an affront to God but injurious to life. The commonly held view is that according to every religion it is a bad thing to sin because, no matter how much it pleases us, it displeases Him. In the Psalms and in prophecy, however, we find a different approach to sin. Thus, while King David, following a major transgression, cries out that "it is only against Thee that I have sinned!" he speaks time and again about the harm that sin has done to himself. Take just one example: in Psalm 38:4–9, David speaks clearly of how sin has sickened him. "There is no soundness in my flesh because of Your indignation; there is no peace in my bones because of my sins. For my iniquities have gone over my head, like an onerous burden; they are too heavy for me. My boils fester until they rot because of my folly. Therefore I cringed and was greatly lowered down. I went about all day with spirits downcast. For my loins are filled with burning and there is no soundness in my flesh. I wasted away and was sorely depressed; I groaned from the moaning of my heart."

It is obvious that the psalmist speaks here, as on various other occasions, of sin as having a sickening effect on body *and* soul. Not only that there is no peace of mind, there is not even peace of body. His spirit is "downcast" and there is no soundness in his "flesh." Is it a matter of Divine on-the-spot punishment for sins? Not at all! Sins are, to a vast degree, self-punishing: "Sins punish the sinner." "Sin is born together with its punishment." The Rav explains it thus: "Sin has [also] a polluting quality. . . . The Jewish view recognizes a state of 'impurity of sin' (*tumat hahet*). The entire Bible abounds in references to this idea of self-pollution, contamination, rolling about in the mire of sin. This impurity makes its mark on the sinner's personality. Sin, as it were, removes the Divine halo from man's head, impairing his spiritual integrity. In addition to the frequent appearance of this idea in Scripture and in the homiletical teachings of the Aggadah, we also find many concrete references to 'impurity of sin' in the Halakhah" ("On Repentance").

SIN AS A DEFECT OF THE SPIRIT

After explaining that according to Halakhah an Israelite who has transgressed suffers a reversal in his legal status and is discredited as a witness in a court of law, the Rav stresses that this demoted state does not constitute further punishment, but is, rather, indicative of a change in the sinner's inner self. "As a result of sin, man is not the same person he was before. Every man is presumed acceptable as a creditable witness. Natural truthfulness is, to my way of thinking, an integral part of man's character. The moment a person sins, however, he lessens his own worth, brings himself down, and becomes spiritually defective, thus forgoing his former status. Sin deprives man of his natural privileges and unique human attributes. He is subjected to a complete transformation as his original personality departs and another one replaces it. This is not a form of punishment, or a fine, and is not imposed in a spirit of anger or vindictiveness. It is a metaphysical corruption of the human personality, being lost and adrift in a vacuum; of spiritual bankruptcy; of frustration and failure. The recovery from sin-sickness is thus a long, difficult process, and only when the penitent undergoes a complete metamorphosis does repentance take place" ("On Repentance").

A complete metamorphosis, which is the only way to overcome metaphysical sin, or the sins which defile, often requires the adoption of a new law of causation—the most difficult part of the *teshuvah* experience, and the most heroic and noble one. Rabbi Adin Steinsaltz elaborates on this in his book on *teshuvah*: "Despite those behavioral laws, there remains *teshuvah*: the ever-present possibility of changing one's life and the very direction of one's life. According to the talmudic sages, this possibility of altering reality after the fact, which is one of the mysteries of all being, was created before the world itself; before the laws of nature came into being—before the mountains were born—as the Divine poet put it, a principle even more fundamental and exalted was proclaimed: that change, *teshuvah*, was possible."

Teshuvah can thus lead to the eradication of symptoms traceable to the past as to an entirely new process of self-recreation in the future. It cannot start, however, "from scratch," but must begin with understanding, or *daat Hashem*. The Rav links his interpretation of *teshuvah* to the biblical corroboration of Proverbs 3:6: "In all thy ways know Him" (not just "acknowledge Him," as it is commonly translated, but "*know Him*"), "and He will straighten out your paths." The Talmud (in Berakhot 53a) describes this passage as "a small portion upon which the whole body of the Torah hangs." The Rav explains what is meant by "know Him": " 'Know Him in all thy ways' [means] in everything thou doest, in every path thou takest, in all situations, under all conditions—'know Him'." "Know Him" means cognition!

The Rav at length describes all possible places, situations, and circumstances in human life in which man can and should know God. This is a kind of knowing which it is impossible to replace with love or faith—love and faith came as a *result* of, not instead of, the right knowing. Contrary to the famous line by Pascal that "our knowledge of God is very far from our love of Him" comes the Rav, going, as he usually does, in the footsteps of Maimonides, and says that "we can only love God with the knowledge we have of Him." Thus the Rav explains: "To believe is necessary, but it is not enough. The Presence of the Almighty must be a personal, intimate experience. . . . If one feels not the touch of His hand, one cannot be a complete Jew." That must have been the numinous experience which the psalmist is speaking about when he says, in words of marvelous simplicity, "Thou hast grasped me by my right hand" (Ps. 73:23).

7

Kant Would Not Have Understood My Grandfather

The Rav could never have made the extraordinarily bold statement that Kant would not have understood his grandfather if he had not been as at home with Kant as he is with the teaching of the Torah.

The Rav has juxtaposed Kant, undoubtedly one of the greatest philosophers of the last two centuries, with his grandfather, Reb Haim, the universally acknowledged Gaon of Brisk, for a very special reason. Kant, just *because* he was a giant of wisdom, unconsciously confirmed, as it were, the maxim of the sages: "There is wisdom among the nations—believe it; there is Torah among the nations—don't believe it" (Eicha Rabbah, chap. 2).

But before we try to explain the Rav's assertion that Kant would not have understood his grandfather, let us talk for a while about Kant. The great German philosopher, one of the most profound thought-innovators in postmedieval philosophy, appeared on the horizon of an awakening Europe where the spirit of criticism, which has for quite some time now undermined authority and tradition, was bringing reason itself to the bar by denying reason's ultimate authority.

In the seventeenth–century, Locke examined the problem of knowledge, or, as it was referred to, "sovereign reason," more thoroughly than had hitherto been attempted. Less than a century later, David Hume drew what appeared to him to be the inevitable consequences of the strictly empirical view of knowledge. In his *An Inquiry Concerning Human Understanding* and other works, he puts forward the argument that if there is nothing in the mind which is not in the senses, or, in other words, if we can only know what we experience in sensation and reflection, then rational theology, rational cosmology, and rational psychology are impossible. The knowledge of God, world, and soul is simply beyond our ken. Even in his more cautious *Treatise*, religious beliefs are noticed only as distorting fundamentally sound principles of human nature.

It was, however, not the empiricist school alone which was weighing rationalism in the balance and finding it wanting. There also arose an opposition to its claim to finality from the camp of the mystics, who distrusted the chilling intellectual prose of the rationalists and craved to still their longing for eternity by what they regarded as the metaphysical dimension of the soul. To a growing number of thinking people, the *unaided* natural intelligence appeared to end either in a hopeless skepticism or in a tragic fatalism that mocks humanity's deepest yearnings and most cherished values.

It was in this atmosphere of great expectations and equally great frustrations that Immanuel Kant's critical and transcendental philosophy made its stunning appearance. Kant, the man who was called the Copernicus of modern philosophy, shook European Enlightenment, along with the rationalism of Descartes and Leibnitz, as well as the empiricism of Locke, Berkeley, and Hume. What was so revolutionary about Kant was that he looked for a theory of knowledge which should thoroughly investigate its own possibilities and limits, and thus make it possible for the human intellect to criticize its own powers and see itself in the mirror of its limitations.

In his three critical works, *The Critique of Pure Reason*, *The Critique of Practical Reason*, and *The Critique of Judgment*, Kant tries to cope with three crucial questions of all thinking men: "What *can* I do? What *ought* I to do? What may I *hope* for?" According to Kant, whose influence on Enlightenment Jewry was exceedingly great, we can never have knowledge, in the scientific sense, of the existence of God, moral freedom, and the immortality of the soul. Human reason can never prove or disprove them. And the reason why they cannot be proved or disproved is because they are not phenomena, but noumena. The term "noumena" refers to "the thing in itself", and human reason cannot see things as they are in themselves, but rather, as they are seen through the colored glasses of space and time. Kant's procedure differed considerably from the empiricist method, for he was concerned with questions which he himself called transcendental, such as: "Under what conditions is experience of an objective world possible?"

Kant did not provide us with an answer to this crucial question, but he provided us, or so he thought, with the necessary, but by no means sufficient, conditions for an *a priori* moral principle, namely, that one should only adopt and act on principles which everyone can adopt. Kant does not tell us, however, which of such principles we *ought* to adopt; his famous categorical imperative is thus best seen not as a source of moral principles, but as a *test* of the principles we already possess.

One of these principles is the moral law. The sense of awe which Kant felt for the moral law he expressed in famous lines at the end of his second *Critique*: "Two things fill the mind with ever new and increasing wonder and awe the oftener and the more steadily we reflect on them: the starry heaven above and the moral law within."

Kant, contrary to his predecessors, admitted even from the razor-sharp angle of his critical philosophy[1] that there may be, beyond the phenomenal world, a world of noumena, that is to say, realities of another order which cannot be perceived and which are inaccessible and consequently superior to anything human reason can ever hope to perceive. From this premise, Kant moves to another one: While pure reason will never be able to prove scientifically the existence of God and the immortality of the soul, our practical reason, that is to say, our moral consciousness, demands them as postulates. Thus, in *The Critique of Practical Reason*, Kant accords a different treatment to the first principles, such as freedom of the will, the existence of God, etc., which in the *Critique of Pure Reason* he regarded as possible, but incapable of proof. In his second major work, he considered them to be defi-

---

1. So sharp and subtle that Marcus Herz, one of his most knowledgeable friends and disciples—a Jew—informed the master halfway through the *Critique* that if he did not stop he would go mad.

nitely postulated on the ground that morality is simply inconceivable without them.

Kant also had a definite attitude toward Judaism. It stems from his idea about the autonomy of the will as expressed in or by the categorical imperative, which amounts to moral self-legislation of the individual. To Kant, autonomy of the will is the sole principle of all moral laws and of all norms and duties which conform with them. What it means, in other words, is that heteronomy of the will—laws or statutes imposed upon a person from the "outside"—not only cannot serve as a basis for any obligation, but, on the contrary, oppose the very principle thereof and, hence, the morality of the will. Kant insisted on moral autonomy to such an extent that he regarded any law imposed upon human beings by an outsider, even if that outsider is God Himself, as valueless unless subjected to the scrutiny of man's own conscience and moral self-legislation. What Kant referred to as the categorical imperative brooks no condition or motive other than the moral law in man himself. Any kind of heteronomy must lead, in his view, to spurious morality.

JUDAISM AS THEONOMY

To say that Judaism, which is a religion of law—*revealed* law, to be sure—is heteronomous is easy. Revelation, after all, come from "without." To understand it, however, as theonomy—Divine law—is impossible without experiencing it as such. The study of the law and the accompanying compliance with it may start as a heteronomous experience. The sages of the Talmud had a word for this: *shelo lishma*—"not for its own sake." They recommend it, however, for out of *shelo lishma* may come *lishma*—"for its own sake."

If the first stage suggests heteronomy, the second, *lishma*, clearly implies autonomy, or, rather, heteronomy experienced as autonomy. This is also the deeper meaning of the wonderful comment by the sages on the biblical passage about the law having been "engraved" (*harut*) on the Tablets: "Read it not," they say, "as *harut*-['engraved'] but as *herut* ['freedom']." What this means is as far-reaching and all-embracing as anything that was ever said on the subject: what was before just "engraved" from without—heteronomous law—now becomes the higher essence of man's craved spiritual and existential freedom—of *ḥerut*. The Rav quotes in this context King David's last words: "So spake the man who was raised on high" (II Sam. 23:1). The word for "high" is *al*, but if you read *ol* instead of *al*—no change in the letters, only in the vowels—it means "So spake the man who was raised by a yoke." A yoke usually bends man down; the yoke of Torah, however, the yoke of the Kingdom of Heaven, lifts up and straightens out.

We should add here that even from Kant's point of view, as one of his later non-Jewish disciples pointed out, there is a serious flaw in the argument that only those actions can be considered moral which are justifiable before the moral conscience of the individual. "If I accept the commandments of God as morally binding for me, I do it because the conception of God includes his attributes as the highest moral Being. It is therefore my own moral will which I have recognized as identical with the will of God, with the commandments of God. I obey at the same time my own moral imperative. . . . I affirm the heteronomous commandment, make it a norm of my own will, and thus I act autonomously although at the beginning I did not carry the norm for my moral action in myself, but it reached me from the outside" (Paul Hensel, *Haupt Problems der Ethics*).

It is generally agreed, more so now than before, that Kant's critical philosophy, which showed the limits of the human mind, was acceptable in part even to traditional Judaism. His moral philosophy, however, particularly his theory of moral autonomy in the sense of moral self-legislation, proved to be an affront to traditional Judaism. The fact that German Reform Judaism used Kantian arguments, so much *en vogue* in those days, to justify its rejection of the Halakhah on *moral* grounds (no more and no less!) was enough to make many a thinking Masoretic Jew count the great philosopher among harmful heretics. On the other hand, no less a halakhic personage than Samson Raphael Hirsch detected something more in Kant than the misuse to which Abraham Geiger, his contemporary and ideologue of Reform, put the categorical imperative. But it was Hirsch's great grandson, Rabbi Yitzhak Breuer, a profound Jewish thinker and outstanding man of Halakhah, who discovered in Kant a dimension of thought which led him to the conclusion that the great philosopher "stands on the threshold of Judaism."

Strange, isn't it? Yet Rabbi Breuer, an authority on Kantian philosophy, was quite convinced, and his argument may be equally convincing. In *Nahaliel* he writes: "Kant stands on the threshold of Judaism, but he proceeds no further than that. Within himself he sensed the universal moral law just as he sensed within himself the universal theoretical law. He was indeed the discoverer of the latter. For the Creator, who created man 'in His image', had endowed him with the ability to recognize that which exists and to dominate it. But Kant did not discover the universal moral law, for the moral universe is not what *is, but what should be*. The conception alone of that universe and the striving for it has been instilled in mankind by the Creator, in order that he, man, may hear, obey, and perfect. Kant *confounded* his yearning for the universal moral law with the law itself and thus arrived at his conception of the autonomy of the human will and the complete negation of the moral heteronomy (of statutes imposed from without), even if it is God that stands for the *Heteros*. . . . Ultimately," Breuer concedes, "it was the serpent that spoke out of his mouth: 'you will be as gods knowing good and evil.' The way of Judaism is completely different. It starts out with the heteronomy of the law, and it leads to an autonomy, to a 'sanctity' which embodies God's will completely in the will of self."

In *The New Kuzari* Rabbi Breuer goes on to elaborate his thesis. As Kant did not know the cosmonomy of the Torah, he writes, he was obliged to proclaim the autonomy of man. "The world in itself, however, is not being molded by our will. It is, rather, the other way round: Our own will is molded by the world in itself. It is only the cosmonomy of the Torah which can redeem our will from the heteronomy of the world in itself. What Kant understood under the autonomy of man vis-à-vis the world of the will is nothing but the idea of the cosmonomy of the Torah. Here lies the fatal error: the idea of cosmonomy is not yet cosmonomy itself! Any attempt on the part of human beings to develop a cosmonomy out of its *idea* cannot succeed. Only the Creator Himself can do this, because only He possesses the full knowledge of the inner essence of the cosmos, whereas the utmost we humans possess is only an *idea* of the cosmos, but not the mystery of the cosmos in creation.''

Thus, even Kant, who must be counted among the greatest philosophers of the Post-Renaissance era, could only remain "on the threshold of Judaism." Why couldn't he step over the threshold? To understand this is to grasp the reason for the Rav's definitive opinion that Kant would not have understood his grandfather. A psalm of extraordinary power and beauty—the nineteenth—may help us clarify our point. We read this psalm, as we do others, with fervor or by rote, but only rarely with a sense of wonder. It often takes an outsider to point out the wonder in what one takes for granted. And the outsider in question is the famous British author, poet, thinker, and seeker, C. S. Lewis.

REFLECTIONS ON A PSALM

Lewis underwent conversion from Protestantism to Catholicism, and most of his books deal with ultimate questions, for to him—extraordinarily sensitive man that he was—even pain was an ultimate question. Lewis's little book *Reflections on the Psalms* contains a chapter which raises all the right questions without necessarily providing the right answers. But there are cases in our quest for truth when answers are not really important if and when juxtaposed with the irresistible grandezza of the questions. This is just one such case. C. S. Lewis, who often fascinates us with his choice of the exact poetic words to define a psalm ("This Psalm," he says about Psalm 119, "was written by a soul ravished by moral beauty"!) is also capable of surprising us with extraordinary flashes of exegetic insight and curiosity.

Psalm 19 is truly a case in point. Undoubtedly "the greatest poem in the Psalter and one of the greatest lyrics in the world," it presents an enigma to Mr. Lewis. He mentions a passage from a tragedy by Racine, "a mighty French poet and steeped in the Bible," titled *Athalie*, in which a chorus of Jewish girls sings an ode about the original giving of the law on Mount Sinai. It has the remarkable refrain of "O, Charmante Loi" (Act I, scene iv). Lewis rightly remarks that the French *charmante* is definitely not the same as "charming" in English, which has come to be a tepid or even patronizing word. "How we should translate 'Charmante' I don't know," Lewis says, " 'Enchanting'? 'delightful'? 'beautiful'? None of them quite fits. What is, however, certain is that Racine is here coming nearer than any modern writer I know to a feeling very characteristic of certain psalms, and it is a feeling which I, at first, found utterly bewildering."

What Lewis found, at first, "utterly bewildering" are the psalmist's ecstatic descriptions at the law: "More to be desired are they [the laws of the Torah] than gold; sweeter also than honey and the honeycomb" (19:10). Lewis comments: "One can well understand this being said of God's mercies, God's visitations, His attributes. But what the poet [the psalmist] is actually talking about is God's law, His commands, His 'rulings'—What is being compared to gold and honey are 'those statutes' which, we are told, 'rejoice the heart' (8), for the whole poem is about the law, not about judgment."

"What is being compared to gold and honey are those statutes . . ." Those statutes, we must assume—must we not?— were "imposed from without," and must therefore be regarded as heteronomous. Yet the psalmist speaks of statutes which deal, as we all know, with what Kant would call "phenomena," as if they were suffused with some dazzling rays of a light that is easily traceable to the numinous. Small wonder, therefore, that they appeared "very mysterious" to Lewis.

He could understand, he says, that man can and must respect and obey statutes like "Thou shall not steal," "Thou shall not commit adultery," etc. But it is very hard, Mr. Lewis avers, "to find how these laws could be, so to speak, delicious, how they exhilarate." If this is difficult at any time, Mr. Lewis argues, it is doubly so when obedience to either is opposed to some strong and perhaps in itself innocent desire. "A man held back by his unfortunate previous marriage to some lunatic or criminal who never dies, from some woman whom he faithfully loves; or a hungry man, left alone, without money, in a shop filled with the smell and sight of new bread, roasted coffee or fresh strawberries—can these find the prohibition of adultery and theft at all like honey? They may obey, they may still respect the statute. But surely it may be more aptly compared to the dentist's forceps or the front line more than anything enjoyable or sweet."

Mr. Lewis's problem gains in strength as he realizes, as he must, that the law in the Psalms does not mean simply the Ten Commandments. "It means the whole complex legislation (religious, moral, civil, criminal, and even constitutional) contained in Leviticus, Numbers, and Deuteronomy. The man who 'pores upon it' is obeying Joshua's command: 'The book of the law shall not depart out of thy mouth, but thou shall meditate therein day and night' (Josh. 1:8)."

The conclusions one reaches, the sensations one experiences, upon "mediating upon it day and night," that is to say, upon a lifetime of involvement in *daat Hashem*, in the study and knowledge of the Torah—the psalmist describes this life-giving pursuit with the irresistible power of words which are more categorical than any categorical imperative: "The law of the Lord is perfect, reviving the soul; the testimony of the Lord is faithful, making wise the simple; the statutes of the Lord are right, rejoicing the heart; the commandments of the Lord are pure, enlightening the eyes. The fear of the Lord is pure, enduring forever; the ordinances of the Lord are truth and righteous altogether. More to be desired are they than gold. Yeah, much more than fine gold; sweeter also than honey and the honeycomb."

The categorical, even ecstatic tone about the everlastingness of the Law, is going hand-in-hand with its acknowledged power to elevate and enchant. This theme of enchanted obedience—for that's the word for it!—occurs time and again in the Psalms. The Psalmist speaks of his "delight" in those statutes (Psalm 16); to study them, he exclaims "is like finding treasures" (Psalm 14); those statutes affect him like music and are his "songs" (Psalm 54). Again, "they taste like honey" (Psalm 103). "They are better than silver or gold" (Psalm 72). These, and many others of the same kind, to quote Lewis again, "is not priggery, nor even scrupulosity. *It is the language of a man ravished by moral beauty.* If we cannot at all share his experience, *we shall be the losers.*"

THE LAW AS FIRMNESS TOUCHED

After these extraordinarily phrased impressions and confessions, Lewis rightly observes that on three occasions in the Psalms the

Divine poet asserts that "the law is true" or that it is "the truth" (Ps. 86, 138, 142). We also find the same in Psalm 3:7, "All Thy commandments are true." A modern logician, Lewis observes, would say that there is something wrong in this description, or definition, of commands as "true." "A law is a command, and to call a command 'true' makes no sense. 'The door is shut' may be true or false, but 'shut the door' can't." How then are we to understand the repeated assertions of the sweet singer of Israel that the law of the Lord is true? Lewis offers a plausible existential explanation. "What it means is that in the law you find the 'real,' or 'correct,' or 'stable,' well-grounded conditions for living. This law answers the question, 'Wherewithall shall a young man cleanse his way?' (Ps. 119:9). The law is then like a lamp, a guide (Ps. 105). When the psalmist calls the directions or rulings of Yahveh 'true,' he is expressing the assurance "that these, and none other, are the 'real' and 'valid' and 'unassailable' ones; that they are based on the very nature of things and the very nature of God." His laws are "good," "sweet," "delightful," and "righteous" because they have an *emet* in them—a truth, an intrinsic validity, a rock-bottom reality being rooted in His own nature—and are therefore as solid as that nature which He has created.[2] Lewis gives here again a very sound existential interpretation of the Psalms when he says that "their delight in the Law is a delight in having touched firmness, like the pedestrian's delight in feeling the hard road beneath his feet after a false short cut has long entangled him in muddy fields."

The law as the "delight in having touched firmness" would be, according to the Rav, what exactly typifies *not* the homo religiosus, whose main yearning is to take off and soar above the "firmness" of our lives, but the halakhic man, who tries to "finitize the Infinite." We have elaborated on this subject in other chapters, but we must not miss the opportunity to place it in the context of the crucial psalm at hand. The feeling we get in this psalm is by no means one of mystical takeoffs, but, so to speak, of existential landings. We are really dealing here with the wonderful sensation of "having touched firmness." One is anything but adrift in the

---

2. The comparison is fascinating. Both Samson Raphael Hirsch and the Rav observe that the same Hebrew word, *ḥok* ("law"), is applied in the Bible both to man and to nature.

clear, crystalline waters of that great hymn, as of the laws and statutes it turns into hymns. Yes, of course: we are dealing here with laws and judgments, with statutes and rulings, but we cannot help the elevating feeling of total *authenticity* it arouses in us. Here, indeed, is the *whole man* whom Ecclesiastes must have had in mind, all his searing moodiness notwithstanding, when he concluded his book with the words, "Fear the Lord and keep His laws, for that is the whole man."

"IF I CANNOT SHARE AT ALL THIS EXPERIENCE . . ."

But Lewis, decent fellow that he was, would not have remained loyal to his newfound conversion if he had let the psalmist "get away," so to speak, with the law—the law which, as we all know, Paul (or Saul) of Tarsus insisted had been invalidated by Jesus. Is it possible, one cannot help wondering, that Paul also had the Nineteenth Psalm in mind when he declared that the law it so exuberantly extolls was no longer valid? Paul may have wished to free people from the yoke of the law, but why deprive them of the delight it brings to its observers?

Mr. Lewis does not come up with a definitive answer. Instead, he falls back, seemingly unsure of himself, on some Pharisee-and-Scribe-bashing arguments, easily traceable to the church fathers, whom Jules Isaac rightly refers to as "teachers of contempt." We shall not repeat these arguments, for their very source is suspect. What is worthy of quoting in this connection is Mr. Lewis's persuasion that there are passages in the Psalms where the law of God appears as truly "undefiled." It is a law which "gives light"; it is "clean," "everlasting," and "sweet." And then Lewis makes his most forceful statement on the subject: "No one can improve on this, and nothing can more fully admit us to the old Jewish feeling about the law: luminous, severe, disinfectant, exultant. . . . If we cannot share all this experience, we shall be the losers" (*Reflections on the Psalms*).

And they shall not be alone. One does not have to be a Christian *not* to share this experience, and one does not have to be a C. S. Lewis to feel what it was. The number of Jews who *do not* share this feeling is legion. For to share this experience is not only a matter of knowing what it says, but of *living* it in truth. In the Lithuanian yeshivot, moreover, particularly in the Musar yeshivot (with which the Rav does not always see eye-to-eye), there prevailed a conviction, easily traceable to Maimonides, that when a person is biased or deficient in character, he cannot fully grasp the Torah no matter how intelligent and learned he is. Thus, a leading Lithuanian master of Musar, Reb Simha Zisl Broide of Kelm, taught that a person had to subject both his presuppositions and his personality to theoretical analysis and concrete means of *tik-kun*, or repair, in order to become a true student of Torah.[3]

The Rav, I am sure, a Litvak himself (Brisk D'Lita!), would readily subscribe to this criterion, and, in fact, he hints at it in "The Halakhic Man" when he comments on a passage in Psalm 119, "I will *delight* myself in Thy commandments which I have loved. . . . This is my comfort in my affliction that Thy word hath quickened me." To this the Rav comments: "We do not have here a directive that imposes upon man obligations against which he rebels, but delightful commandments which his soul passionately desires. . . . When halakhic man comes to the real world, he has already created his ideal, a priori image, which shines with the radiance of the norm."

THE LAWS OF THE LORD ARE CLEAR

It is no coincidence that the Rav uses a passage from the self-same Nineteenth Psalm, "The laws of the Lord are clear, enlightening the soul," as the motto of his remarkable essay on his grandfather's way of teaching. The ability of Rabbi Haim of Brisk to unravel the intricacies of the law and make them not just clear but outrightly luminous to his students was his lasting contribution to the new way of Torah study. Under the majestic sway of this mode of learning, one experienced not only the pleasure of an obscure halakhic problem being illuminated, but of a path of life merging into a royal highway. It was not only a solution to a problem of law, but an elucidation of a problem of existence. It was, in fact, an existential experience par excellence.

---

3. See Hillel Goldberg, *The Fire Within*.

"The light that shone forth from his teaching," says the Rav, "radiated a special splendor." When this "special splendor" is descriptive not of "God's mercies," as Lewis puts it, or of "his visitations," but of "His ruling, His statutes, His commands," then we clearly are dealing here with phenomena experienced as noumena. Kant would not have understood Reb Haim of Brisk because no philosopher as philosopher, not even the greatest among them, would be able to discover numinous qualities in the phenomena of the law. C. S. Lewis could not understand the crucial psalm for the very same reason that Immanuel Kant could not understand the Rav's grandfather!

WHY DO JEWS HAVE SEPARATE PURE FORMS?

But why go so far? Prof. Eugene Borowitz, a liberal Jewish theologian, wrote a book titled *A New Jewish Theology in the Making* (as if there ever were such a thing as an "old" Jewish theology; the Halakhah, like the Bible, is, as mentioned, *not* theology, but theonomy!). Now let us see what Prof. Borowitz has to say in that book about the Rav's concept of the halakhic man. "A Christian might well argue, if the halakhic man is a pure type— and if he is a particularly Jewish type, why do Jews have separate pure forms?—Must the halakhic man necessarily be a Jew? It is clear that Protestant Christians would rarely fall under such a typology, but almost all the characteristics mentioned of the halakhic man could easily be applied to personality types well known in Roman Catholicism, particularly in the Jesuit order."

This, to say the least, is an astonishing statement. For none of the characteristics mentioned by the Rav of the halakhic man could possibly apply to personality types "well known in Roman Catholicism, particularly in the Jesuit order."

The founder of the Jesuit order, who is to this day its ideal symbol and saint, was Ignatius Loyola, a sixteenth-century Christian mystic whose religious imagination was as great as his organizational genius. He penned in a few short lines his ideal of the obedient Jesuit: "Altogether, I must not desire to belong to myself, but to my Creator and to His representative. I must let myself be led and moved as a lamp of wax lets itself be kneaded. I must be as a dead man's corpse without will or judgment; as a little crucifix which lets itself be moved without difficulty from one place to another; as a staff in the hand of an old man, to be placed where he wishes and where he can best make use of me. Thus, I must always be ready to hand, so that the Creator may use me and apply me in the way that to him seems good'' (from Malachi Martin, *The Jesuits*).

Compare this to the way the Rav defines the halakhic man, nay, the way the halakhic man has appeared for centuries as the role model of a man whom God has placed in this world in order to serve as a pillar of its existence. The Rav speaks of the "autonomy of the intellect" of the halakhic man which "at times reaches heights unimaginable in any other religion." Contrary to the ideal Jesuit, the halakhic man "approaches the world of Halakhah with his mind and intellect, just as cognitive man approaches the natural realm." Halakhic man, moreover, "is not particularly submissive and retiring, and is not meek when it is a matter of maintaining his own views. Neither modesty nor humility characterizes the image of the halakhic man. On the contrary, his most characteristic feature is strength of mind. . . . He recognizes no authority other than the authority of the intellect (obviously, in accordance with the principles of tradition)."

The halakhic man, the Rav asserts, received the Torah from Sinai not as a simple recipient, but as a creator of worlds, as a partner with the Almighty in the act of creation. So great and marvelous is this partnership that the sages of the Talmud speak of cases of controversies in matters pertaining to the interpretation of the law in which the heavenly court tried to mediate, but lo! "the earthly court decrees and the Holy One, blessed be He complies! If the earthly court (which derives its authority from God's Torah) rules in matter of law and judgment, the Halakhah is always in accordance with its decision, even if the heavenly court should disagree" ("The Halakhic Man").

MUST THE HALAKHIC MAN NECESSARILY BE A JEW?

Dr. Borowitz must have had the homo religiosus in mind, but by no means the halakhic man, when he spoke of similar "characteristics" among the Jesuits. But even if he meant the homo religiosus, it is highly doubtful whether the Jewish homo religiosus is similar in his characteristics to his non-Jewish counterpart. A liberal theologian of considerable sagacity and familiarity with both, Dr. Leo Baeck, in his last great statement of German liberal Judaism, has this to say about the singularity of the Jewish homo religiosus: "The religion of this people [Israel], in which its genius matured, in which alone it could flourish, is marked by a unique concept: human existence elevated into the realm of the task and the chosenness of man. Everything given to man in his existence *becomes a commandment.* All that he has received means 'Thou shalt!' The word 'life' acquired a different content from that it received in other cultures."

What this means is the thought which Franz Rosenzweig held up as a flag of Torah Judaism: "And eternal life He planted in our midst." How? The very notion of the Torah as a Torah of life, and we mean life as an affirmation thereof, runs contrary to anything that any religious recluse, no matter how pure, has ever believed in. The Jews have "separate pure forms" without at all denying other kinds of pure forms to others because they, and they alone, have embraced not just a Halakhah, but indeed a halakhic life order which affirms existence as a pursuit of creativity.

Must the halakhic man necessarily be a Jew? A non-Jew, a Catholic like C. S. Lewis, provided the answer when he said, speaking of the original Torah Jew as preconceived by the psalmist, that "if we cannot share all this experience we shall be the losers." So, it seems, will Dr. Borowitz.

THE COMPANY HE KEEPS

The company which the halakhic man keeps consists of other halakhic men who are alive with him though they died a thousand years ago. The halakhic man, who never wished to acquire the characteristic of genuine Christian piety, namely, "ascension to a bodiless spirit, God," but, to the contrary, *to bring God down to earth*, never sought deliverance from this world; he craved to redeem it by first redeeming himself. And it is precisely in this context of purely Christian notion of ascension to or deliverance from, that the question begs itself whether anybody under any circumstance can ever experience anything like "being delivered from" when the delivery in question happens to be from a kind of teaching which is experienced as "sweeter than honey and more precious than gold"?

Here, it seems, Paul, the deliverer from the law, and Immanuel Kant, the apostle of the moral law within, find themselves stuck, as it were, on the threshold of Judaism, the difference being only this: the first was on his way out and locked the door behind him. The second did not have or could not find a key to the door. The two, however, were not very far apart philosophically. The distance between the Kantian moral law within and Paul's categorical insistence that the law was fulfilled forever after in Jesus of Nazareth is not very great. It is no accident that Protestantism saw in Kant—and Kant in Protestantism—something or somebody to hold on to.

But let us go back for a moment to "the old Jewish feeling about the law." The word "old" is undoubtedly meant to raise the question whether the feelings which the psalmist expressed about the law almost a millennium prior to Christianity are in any way different from what the halakhic man would feel about it today.

The Rav's answer bears repeating. As we mentioned in an earlier chapter, he speaks of the chain of tradition, which began millennia ago, and will continue till the end of time. Time, the Rav avers, is not, in this conception, destructive and all-consuming, and it does not consist of fleeting, imperceptible moments. "This wonderful chain which originated on that bright morning of the day of Revelation and which stretches forward into the eschaton, represents the manner in which the Jewish people experience their own history, a history that floats upon the stormy waters of time. The consciousness of the halakhic man, that master of the received tradition, embraces the entire company of the sages of the Mishnah. He lives in their midst, discusses and argues questions of Halakhah with them, delves into and analyzes fundamental halakhic principles in their company. All of them merge into one time experience. He walks alongside Maimonides, listens to Rabbi Akiba, senses the presence of Abaye and Raba. He rejoices with them and shares in their sorrow." Here there is no ascension to a bodiless spirit, God. Here, there is descent; the Lord God is brought down, as it were, to earth, as it is written, "and the Lord descended in the cloud" (Exod. 34:5). No, no ascension to God "for The Lord thy God walketh in the midst of thy camp" (Deut. 23:15). It is, as the Rav puts it, the contraction of infinity within a finitude bound by laws, measures, and standards, the appearance of transcendence within empirical reality. Ascension to God is an afterlife proposition, an ascent at the end of empirical reality.

The lowering of transcendence into the midst of our turbid, coarse, material world can take place only through the implementation of the ideal Halakhah in the core of reality. The entire Halakhah is not only a creative exercise, but an exercise in creation. The very notion of *hiddushei Torah*, "new insights into the Torah," bespeaks an ongoing process of creativity—primarily the creativity involved in man's creating himself. "The power of creative interpretation (*hiddushim*) is the very foundation of the received tradition" ("The Halakhic Man"). Commenting on the passage "Thou didst fashion me after and before" (Ps. 139:5), the Rav quotes Rabbi Ishmael ben Tanhum: "After all the actions and before all the punishment. . . . If he proves worthy, we say of him, 'you preceded creation', as it is written; 'And the spirit of God (i.e., man) hovered over the face of the waters' (Gen. 1:2). But if not—'a gnat preceded you, a snail preceded you!' " Herein, says the Rav, is embodied the entire task of creation and the obligation to participate in the renewal of the cosmos. The most fundamental principle of them all is that man must create himself. It is this idea that Judaism introduced into the world." It thus follows that "the peak of religious ethical perfection which Judaism aspires is man as creator."

The idea of man the creator, or co-creator with God the Creator, implies not just creativity, but an actual human need for inner growth. "I don't think I could have stood the pain of non-growing in me. I just couldn't" is a line I came across somewhere and cannot forget. I know of a case of a noted man of Halakhah, a dying man, who, upon awakening from a coma and noticing his brother-in-law, who was his partner in study also a noted man of Halakhah, at his side, asked "A new insight, my friend?" The insight he was asking about was what the Rav means by *hiddushei torah*, which are, existentially speaking, "stages of growth." The halakhic man had a word—a Yiddish word—for these stages: *shteigen in lernen*, "growing in study."

The Rav speaks a good deal about the autonomy of the intellect which reaches in the Halakhah "heights unimaginable in any other religion." The Rav, as mentioned, refers to the cases in the Talmud where interference by the Heavenly Court in matters in Halakhah under discussion among the grandees of the law is clearly resented by the human participants, and the Heavenly Court yields. "The Torah is not in heaven" is a formidable and incomparable thought which comes to mean that once the Divine law has descended to earth and is subjected to the majority decision of earthly men, qualified to pronounce judgment, it must be left to them to decide according to the a priori law. The *talmid ḥakham* is thus regarded by the sages as higher than the angels. The exultation of the truly great is boundless in Judaism. "Halakhic man," the Rav writes, "reigns over all and is esteemed by all. No other cognitive discipline has woven a crown for its heroes to the extent that the Halakhah has done. In no other field of knowledge has man been adorned with the crown of absolute royalty as in the realm of Torah. The glorification of man reaches here the peak of splendor" ("The Halakhic Man").

THE CROWN OF ABSOLUTE ROYALTY

Does this mean that the halakhic man is a nondialectical personality—a man in whom the eternal clash between life and the spirit has been reconciled? The Rav himself argues that Judaism knows only the thesis and the antithesis. The famous Hegelian synthesis is a matter of eschatological fulfillment. How come, then, that we get the feeling, studying "The Halakhic Man" and "The Halakhic Mind," that we are dealing here with a personality in whom the inevitable gap between life and the spirit has been bridged?

The question has been widely discussed in recent years, but the answer, in our view, is simply this: that the halakhic man is a dialectical personality because in addition to being a "pure" halakhic type, he is also a general homo-religiosus type of man. What this actually means is that while the homo religiosus is not necessarily a halakhic man, the halakhic man is inevitably and invariably a homo religiosus. The dialectical clash here is thus even more pronounced than in other cases of homo religiosus: the very fact that the Halakhah tries to bridge the gap—never abolish but bridge it—between life and the spirit, intensifies the inner conflict of the homo religiosus *even* as a halakhic man! The talmudic adage "The greater the man, the stronger his sinful urge" must, in our view, be understood in this context.

HALAKHIC MAN TODAY

The picture of the halakhic man would not be complete without our seeing him the way he was seen by Jews who were not necessarily halakhic men. Here we come across a phenomenon which confirms the Rav's above-mentioned contention that "no other cognitive discipline has woven a crown for its heroes to the extent that the halakhic man has done." That crown, however, was woven not only by the grandeur of the discipline itself, but by a people who came to intuitively, almost instinctively, feel that there was something akin to majesty about the *talmid ḥakham* in their midst. The life story of the Rav himself bears witness to the sense of reverence, admiration, and indeed, adoration which thousands of people feel for this towering halakhic personality. The quality of "festive dignity" which the Rav attributes to the halakhic man is precisely what typifies the halakhic man par excellence—the Rav.

Ludwig Lewisohn is perfectly right when he says that "in the long, illiterate ages of Europe when a priest who could half-read his missal was considered a great scholar, the Jews had made of a book a living substitute for their lost fatherland."[4] They made it even more so in the much-maligned Eastern European Jewish shtetl, where *lerenen*, which is, we must not forget, a much more telling word than "learning," was tantamount to being—the kind of being in the world which counted infinitely more than having.

---

4. Lewisohn, in his *The American Jew*, quotes the following from S. M. Blumenfeld's *Masters of Troyes*: "A Christian of the 12th century wrote: 'A Jew, however poor, if he had ten sons, would put them all to letters, not for gain, as the Christians do, but for the understanding of God's law and not only his sons, but his daughters, too!' "

One does not have to look in Hasidic literature for authentic descriptions of the role which the halakhic man, the *talmid ḥa-kham*, played in the shtetl. A book written by two sociologists, Mark Zborovsky and Elizabeth Herzog, titled *Life Is with People*, tells a good part of the story. Without reference to the axiomatic Hebrew thought, so dear to the Rav, that man was created to create himself, i.e., to complete creation, they write: "[In the shtetl] a Jew without learning is incomplete. He is an ignoramus, an *am haaretz*, and an ignoramus is the most despised member of the community. There is a saying in the Talmud, 'Better a learned bastard than an ignorant priest.' . . . The rank order of Jews with regard to their quality as Jews would approximate their rank order in learning."

A *talmid ḥakham*, they write, "is easily recognizable in the streets of the shtetl. He walks slowly, sedately, absorbed in his thoughts. His speech is calm, rich in quotations from the Bible or the Talmud, allusive and laconic—his words, as they say, are 'counted like pearls.' Not only the poor, but also the wealthy greet him first, if they are less learned. A learned man is a man of noticeable retirement. He seldom laughs aloud; excessive laughter, like any sort of excess, is considered the mark of the *am ha'aretz*. He will react to a joke or a witty saying by a smile or a very short and restrained laugh. . . . The *talmid ḥakham* must indicate his dignity and sophistication by his behavior and his appearance."

The secular authors of the book, contrary to the literary detractors of the shtetl, also noticed something vital, interior, soulful, which outsiders rarely do: the connection between *lernen* and refinement of character! To the halakhic men this was a natural consequence; refinement of character is, after all, regarded by the sages as the gateway to truth. And though the Rav does not feel any special love for Nietzsche, it was he who said in truth that "the truth eludes the person whose mode of thinking is base." The *talmid ḥakham* would wholeheartedly subscribe to this maxim.

"It is assumed that a learned man will be a good husband and father. . . . One of the basic principles of Jewish education is that the mere fact of learning the rules of behavior, which are the commandments of God, causes one to behave in accordance with them. The assumption implies a native desire to know the will of God and a native inclination to obey it. All that is required is the opportunity to discover, through pious and unceasing study, the true import of the commandments.''

Equally elucidating is the part of the book which deals with *shayne yiden*, that is to say, "beautiful Jews." We know what it means when people in America speak of the "beautiful people," and it should be quite obvious that the two notions of beautiful are light years apart. We are all too familiar with the conventional social life that pervades the yawning gulf of meaninglessness, emptiness, and pretense out of which emerges the dreadfully exteriorized show-off celebrity whom the social neophytes are so desperately eager to rub shoulders or take pictures with. We are also familiar with the kind of bejeweled, smiling, name-dropping celebrity worshipping "dah-lings" who qualify in the press and in the media as "beautiful people."

In the poor shtetl, however, where, in the words of the late Nobel laureate Prof. Zalman Waxman, "the material poverty was beyond description and the spiritual riches beyond imagination," it took something else to qualify as "beautiful people." Perhaps the most generally used term to denote those who qualify for the "social register" of the poor shtetl was *shayne yiden*—the fine, literally beautiful Jews. This use of the word "beautiful" to denote other than physical or material attributes is characteristic of a people for whom intangibles have—or have had—a concrete reality. Thus one speaks of "a beautiful deed" or a "beautiful event." To call a house *shayn* does not mean that its exterior is pleasing to the eye, but that the household is dignified and harmonious. Those who excel in generosity are sometimes said to "beautify" the orphan or the pauper. Obscene language, on the other hand, is referred to as "ugly words," and he who uses it is a *grober yung*.

Ideally, the *shayne yiden* possess both learning and wealth. However, while a man of great learning, a *talmid ḥakham* belongs automatically to the *shayne yiden*, a rich man who is an ignoramus is only rated as *shayn* if he makes up with charity what he lacks in learning.

PROSTE YIDEN

It is one of the lasting attributes of the genius of the Jewish people that it developed an attitude of either outright contempt or profound pity for those who knew nothing of—or worse, didn't care to know—what *lernen* is all about. And we speak, as mentioned, of *proste yiden*, which is not the same as *poshute yiden*. The latter, quite often favorite subjects of the Hasidic folktale, are simple, humble, God-fearing Jews who regard their ignorance as something to be ashamed of.

The man who is manifestly *prost*, however, remains so in the eyes of the people even if he is rich. He is uncouth, inconsiderate, ill-mannered, given to unseemly language and at times to what was referred to in the shtetl as "un-Jewish behavior." "To brand a person 'un-Jewish' in the shtetl," the authors rightly observe, "carries the same kind of rebuke as the term 'un-American.' It means not only divergency from the group pattern, but also a falling away from the values and standards considered noblest and best."

There were also other kinds of *proste yiden*: those who, aware of their *prostkeit*, were eager at least to be close to *talmidei hakhamim*, as if there were something therapeutic about their very presence. The learned men, at the same time, out of compassion for these humble *amei ha'aretz*—the arrogant *amei ha'aretz* were treated as outcasts—would often make it a point to study aloud in the bet medrash, where the *proste yiden* would gather to listen and maybe even to learn something. Anyone who ever watched a group of *proste yiden* standing in the back of the house of study on a Saturday afternoon, listening as if their lives depended on it while the local *talmidei hakhamim* engaged in a heated discussion about some difficult question of the law, will always remember the expression of envious admiration and embarrassed helplessness on the faces of the humble *proste yiden* looking on in pained silence.

What such *proste yiden* and *shayne yiden* had in common was the reverence they felt and demonstrated toward the learned men in their midst. Sometimes they would recognize the sage just by his appearance. Thus the renowned *talmid hakham* Prof. Saul Leiberman tells the story of his walking together with his illustrious uncle, a *talmid hakham* of patriarchial appearance, through the Jewish section of Minsk prior to World War I. It was the business district of the city, and many Jewish merchants were sitting outside their stores, waiting for customers. As the sage, whom they did not know, passed by, the merchants, one after the other, rose to their feet. Forming long lines on both sides of the street, they accorded to the sage and his young companion the treatment usually reserved for royalty.

But a most telling case-history about the marvelous and moving attempts of *poshute,* if not *proste, yiden* to resemble or emulate—albeit in some minor way—the *talmid ḥakham* was told by Prof. Leiberman in a lecture he delivered in 1949 before the Rabbinical Assembly of America. During World War I, a German intelligence officer, stationed in Warsaw, heard some rumors about something very mysterious and suspicious going on in the Jewish quarter. It was said that at a certain hour Jewish coachmen would arrive, one after another, without passengers, and disappear for an hour or so in a large courtyard. The German officer went to investigate and, sure enough, there it was: one coachman after another drove his empty carriage into the vast courtyard and disappeared in one of the upper stories of the building. He followed them. What he saw before him was startling: two long tables surrounded by coachmen in their high hats, bent over books and listening attentively to a bearded man who must have been their teacher. It was later explained to the German officer that Jewish coachmen gathered every day at a certain hour to study the law. The German couldn't quite understand it. "It is amazing," he later told his fellow officers, "it is unthinkable; it is inconceivable that German drivers, whose intellectual level is higher than that of Jewish coachmen in Warsaw, would come every day to the University of Berlin to listen to lectures on law!"

One must assume, of course, that the law which the simple coachmen studied for a while every day was a brief, codified "concentrate" of the law, like the popular *Ḥayyei Adam.* That is to say, a compilation of "dry" legalisms at their "dryest," something that makes their eager flocking to where they could study it every day even more astounding. The German officer was absolutely right when he said that German drivers in Berlin were intellectually on a higher level than Jewish coachmen in Warsaw. What he didn't—what he couldn't—understand was that the law, even to some Jewish coachmen in Warsaw, who must have basked in the glow of some *talmid ḥakham,* was a law of *life,* while the law that could be studied at a Berlin university was a law—a professionally studied law—conducive to making a *living.* The

German officer in Warsaw could not understand the Jewish coach-men for almost the same reason that Kant, according to the Rav, would not have understood his grandfather.

A THEONOMY OF PATHOS

C. S. Lewis, as mentioned, raised that famous question about the Nineteenth Psalm: whether man, as the psalm suggests, can really get ecstatic about the law. The answer, however, is given not only in the words of the extraordinary psalm, but in their hermeneutical application and experiential elevation. The Rav, a most complex personality, to be sure, can switch, as he does—maybe precisely on account of his complexity—from the gloom of the Twenty-second Psalm to the supreme yet calm joy of the Twenty-third, and speak of the Halakhah as of an existentially lived poesy: "From the midst of the order and lawfulness [of the Halakhah] we hear a new song, the song of the creature to the Creator, the song of the cosmos to its Maker. Not only the qualitative light, perceptible to the senses, with its wealth of hues and shades, its whirl of colors, sings to the Holy One, blessed be He. So do the quantitative light-waves as well, the fruit of cognitive man's knowledge. Not only the qualitative world bursts forth in song, but so does the quanti-tative world. From the very midst of the laws there arises a cosmos more splendid and beautiful than all the works of Leonardo da Vinci and Michelangelo. . . . Perhaps these experiences of cogni-tive man are lacking in the emotional dynamic and turbulent passion of aesthetic man; perhaps these experiences are devoid of flashy and externally impressive bursts of ecstasy, or psychic enthusiasm. However, they are possessed of profound depth and a clear, penetrating vision. They do not flourish and then fade away like experiences that are only based upon a vague, obscure mo-ment of psychic upheaval. Such an experience is not some fleeting, unstable phenomenon that ebbs and flows, but is fixed and deter-mined, possessed of a clear, and firmly established countenance of its own" ("The Halakhic Man").

THE WORLD AS A WHOLE IS A VERY NARROW RIDGE

Does the Rav mean to say that the halakhic man can lay claim to real peace of mind? Not at all! Whoever studies the Rav's thought is aware that to him "peace of mind" as mentioned is a misnomer: it is either peace *or* mind, and one cannot have both. There is, however, an underlying ontological conviction in the Rav's thought that the halakhic man is infinitely closer, in his relentless quest for creating himself by means of *hiddushei Torah*—new insights in the Torah and, consequently, in himself—than the homo religiosus to a meaning and purpose in life. The Halakhah, as interpreted by the Rav, assumes the nature of an existential, not just a religious, blueprint for a life fully lived. The homo religiosus can, of course, possess the gropings for such a state, but that state may be lacking in steadfastness. Thus the so-called peace of mind which he may temporarily achieve—the Rav regards it as a misnomer—may also be only in the nature of flareups. The *talmid ḥakham*, by contradistinction, is the epitome of steadfastness even when he permits the halakhah to rob him of his enjoyment in studying the Torah. Enjoyment, by the way, must never be confused with peace of mind. The passage in the Psalms "If Thy Torah were not my enjoyment I would have been lost in my misery" (Ps. 119:92) could not have been uttered by a man who knew peace of mind.

We mentioned the possibility of the Halakhah robbing one of his enjoyment of the Torah, and we should explain ourselves. There is a well-known story about the Gaon of Vilna, as told by his illustrious pupil Reb Haim of Volozhin (to whom the Soloveichik family is related). One Friday, the Gaon's servant came to Reb Haim with the message that his master wanted to see him as a matter of great urgency. When Reb Haim came into the Gaon's house, he found him lying in bed with a compress on his head and looking quite ill. The Gaon's wife reported to Reb Haim that it was more than three days since her husband had eaten anything, and that he had hardly enjoyed any sleep all this time. This misery, as Reb Haim soon found out, was caused by his not having been able to understand some difficult passages in the Talmud Yerushalmi. The Gaon now asked his famous pupil to resume the research with him, for is not it written that "two are better than one"? When the two men succeeded in getting the true meaning of the passage, the Gaon recovered instantly, and there was no end to his joy.

Not to be able to go into the depth of a subject, to miss the truth embedded in a single passage, was something which would have caused pain not only to a man of the Gaon's stature. It was enough to watch yeshiva students at Slobodka or Telz or Kelm, passionately involved in halakhic discussions as if their lives depended on it, to know the pain of missing the true meaning of a halakhah and the joy of finding it. The halakhah in question may very well have dealt with the laws of weights and measurements, but the final elucidation of that halakhah had the power of illuminating existence. If the Torah is God-given to man so that he may solve its mysteries, each riddle solved is an experience of a closer partnership with the Universal Lawgiver.

But this joyful experience of a closer partnership with the Universal Lawgiver can only be as sporadic as rare insights. Of course, the Rav says, we invoke with all our hearts the soul-restoring psalm "The Lord is my shepherd." However, this psalm only describes the ultimate destination of homo religiosus, not the path leading to that destination. For the path that will eventually lead to the "green pastures" and to the "still waters" is not "the royal road, but a narrow, twisting footway that threads its course along the steep mountain slope as the terrible abyss yawns at the traveler's feet" ("The Halakhic Man").

In the Rav's words, we hear echoes of the fear and trembling which gripped all great existentialists at the sight of the abyss below and the narrow ridge overhanging it. Kierkegaard spoke of the great leap—over the abyss; Buber, of the "narrow ridge," and Rabbi Nachman of Bratzlav even composed a song about it:

> The world as a whole
> Is a very narrow ridge
> A very narrow ridge!
> And the main thing
> And the main thing
> Is not to fear, not to fear at all!

We said earlier that we are more inclined to think of the halakhic man in anthropological than in typological categories. We base this assumption not only on the halakhic man's unique place in the evolving of the Jewish spirit, but on the extent to which his existence has helped mold the entire sociocultural, let alone religious, consciousness of Jewry for many generations. We are dealing here with a person—the halakhic man—who drew his power not from any official position, but from the quiet depths of his learning. The halakhic man did not always have to teach in order to be followed. Very often he would prefer solitude to any public exposure. But so great was the radiance emitted by what the Rav refers to as "the intellect, the will, feeling, the whole process of self-creation, all proceeding in an ethical direction," that the halakhic man's ethical perfection compelled entire communities to look up to him as to a guiding spirit.

A secular Israeli author, Amos Oz, has asked why we know so little about it if it is true that in the poor Eastern European shtetl, nobody was permitted to go hungry or sleep in the street, crime was unknown, and ignorance was regarded as a sin.

If we know so little about something that was manifest in the social realm, why wonder that we know even less about something that was extant in the much less manifestable realm of the spirit? If Judaism, as someone once said, is the best-kept secret in the world, the next-best-kept secret concerns the personality of the halakhic man—the bearer of the secret. Maybe a day will come when the study of the personality of the halakhic man will become part-and-parcel of the study of the Halakhah. The Rav did it in "The Halakhic Man" in a grand manner. When the sages of the Talmud stress the need for being in the company of *talmidei ḥakhamim* even for the sake of their idle talk, they spoke out of a conviction which Yehudah Halevi gave expression to in the *Kuzari* (pt. 5): "For the Divine law confers something of the nature of angels on the human mind, something which cannot be acquired otherwise."

Bibliography

Arnold, Matthew. *Complete Prose Works*. Ann Arbor, 1960.

Baeck, Leo. *The Essence of Judaism*. New York, 1961.

Barrett, William. *Irrational Man*. Garden City, 1962.

Berdyaev, Nicholas. *The Fate of Man*. New York, 1960.

———*Slavery and Freedom*. New York, 1944.

Buber, Martin. *The Prophetic Faith*. New York, 1949.

Becker, Ernst. *Denial of Death*. New York, 1973.

Camus, Albert. *The Stranger*. New York, 1946.

———*The Plague*. New York, 1948.

———*The Myth of Sisyphus and Other Essays*. New York, 1955.

Cox, Harvey. *The Secular City*. New York, 1966.

Dostoevsky, Fyodor. *Brothers Karamazov*. New York, 1973.

Ellul, Jacques. *Hope in Time of Abandonment*. New York, 1981.

Frankl, Viktor. *The Doctor and the Soul*. New York, 1965.

Glatzer, Nahum. *Franz Rosenzweig*. New York, 1961.

Halevi, Yehudah. *Kuzari*. New York, 1963.

Heidegger, Martin. *Being and Time*. New York, 1962.

James, William. *Essays in Faith and Morals*. Cleveland, 1962.

———*Essays in Religion and Morality*. Cambridge, 1982.

Jaspers, Karl. *Man in the Modern Age*. Chicago, 1961.

Kant, Immanuel. *Critique of Pure Reason*. London, 1964.

———*Critique of Practical Reason*. Chicago, 1960.

———*Critique of Judgment*. Oxford, 1952.

Karo, Yosef. *Shulkhan Arukh*. New York, 1965.

Katz, Steven. *Jewish Ideas and Concepts*. New York, 1977.

———*Jewish Philosophers*. New York, 1975.

Kierkegaard, Soren. *Either-Or*. Garden City, 1962.

Lewis, C. S. *Reflections on the Psalms*. New York, 1958.

Lewisohn, Ludwig. *The Island Within*. New York, 1928.

———*The Creative Life*. New York, 1969.

Locke, John. *An Inquiry Concerning Human Understanding*. Oxford, 1979.

Maimonides, Moses. *Commentary on Avot*. New York, 1977.

Marcel, Gabriel. *The Philosophy of Existentialism*. New York, 1956.

Martin, Malachi. *The Jesuits*. New York, 1987.

Maslow, Abraham. *Religions, Values and Peak Experiences*. Columbus, 1964.

May, Rollo. *Love and Will*. New York, 1969.

Needleman, Jacob. *Sacred Tradition and Present Need*. New York, 1975.

Rank, Otto. *Beyond Psychology*. New York, 1958.

———*The Double*. New York, 1971.

Sartre, Jean-Paul. *Existentialism*. New York, 1953.

Soloveitchik, Joseph B. *Halakhic Man*. Philadelphia, 1983.

Styron, William. *Darkness Visible*. New York, 1990.

Tillich, Paul. *The Courage to Be*. New Haven, 1952.

Tolstoy, Leo. *The Death of Ivan Illich*. New York, 1981.

Valery, Paul. *Selected Works*. New York, 1956.

Zborovsky, Mark. *Life is With People: The Culture of the Shtetl*. New York, 1952.